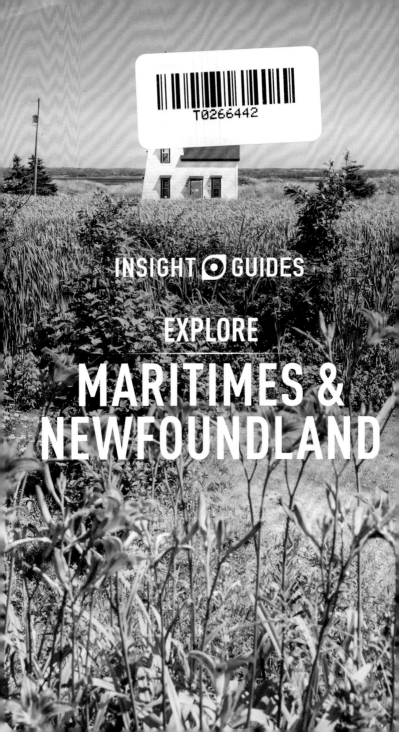

T0266442

INSIGHT ⊙ GUIDES

EXPLORE

MARITIMES &
NEWFOUNDLAND

PROMOTIONAL FEATURE

PLAN & BOOK
YOUR TAILOR-MADE TRIP

BRAZIL **CHILE** **ECUADOR**

TAILOR-MADE TRIPS & UNIQUE EXPERIENCES CREATED BY LOCAL TRAVEL EXPERTS AT INSIGHTGUIDES.COM/HOLIDAYS

Insight Guides has been inspiring travellers with high-quality travel content for over 45 years. As well as our popular guidebooks, we now offer the opportunity to book tailor-made private trips completely personalised to your needs and interests.
By connecting with one of our local experts, you will directly benefit from their expertise and local know-how, helping you create memories that will last a lifetime.

HOW INSIGHTGUIDES.COM/HOLIDAYS WORKS

STEP 1

Pick your dream destination and submit an enquiry, or modify an existing itinerary if you prefer.

STEP 2

Fill in a short form, sharing details of your travel plans and preferences with a local expert.

STEP 3

Your local expert will create your personalised itinerary, which you can amend until you are completely satisfied.

STEP 4

Book securely online. Pack your bags and enjoy your holiday! Your local expert will be available to answer questions during your trip.

PROMOTIONAL FEATURE

BENEFITS OF PLANNING & BOOKING AT
INSIGHTGUIDES.COM/HOLIDAYS

PLANNED BY LOCAL EXPERTS
The Insight Guides local experts are hand-picked, based on their experience in the travel industry and their impeccable standards of customer service.

SAVE TIME & MONEY
When a local expert plans your trip, you save time and money when you book, even during high season. You won't be charged for using a credit card either.

TAILOR-MADE TRIPS
Book with Insight Guides, and you will be in complete control of the planning process, from the initial selections to amending your final itinerary.

BOOK & TRAVEL STRESS-FREE
Enjoy stress-free travel when you use the Insight Guides secure online booking platform. All bookings come with a money-back guarantee.

WHAT OTHER TRAVELLERS THINK ABOUT TRIPS BOOKED AT INSIGHTGUIDES.COM/HOLIDAYS

Trip to Portugal

Every step of the planning process and the trip itself was effortless and exceptional. Our special interests, preferences and requests were accommodated resulting in a trip that exceeded our expectations.

Corinne, USA

Trip to Vietnam

The organization was superb, the drivers professional, and accommodation quite comfortable. I was well taken care of! My thanks to your colleagues who helped make my trip to Vietnam such a great experience.

Heather

DON'T MISS OUT
BOOK NOW AT
INSIGHTGUIDES.COM/HOLIDAYS

CONTENTS

COVID-19 Updates

While travelling in Canada, be sure to heed
all local laws, travel advice and hygiene
measures. While we've done all we can to
make sure this guide is accurate and up to
date, be sure to check ahead.

ART LOVERS

Artistic highlights in this region include the Art Gallery of Nova Scotia in Halifax (route 9) and the Rooms in St John's (route 1), both of which holds collections of fine art.

RECOMMENDED ROUTES FOR...

CHILDREN

Go whale spotting in Twillingate (route 5) or St Anthony (route 7) in Newfoundland, or get educated at the Johnson Geo Centre in St John's (route 1), or the Discovery Centre in Halifax (route 9). Enjoy a day at the beach on Prince Edward Island (both route 13).

FOODIES

Munch your way around Atlantic Canada at the Halifax Seaport Farmers' Market (route 1), or City Market in Saint John (route 14). Sample some of the world's best lobster on PEI (route 13), in New Brunswick (route 15), and Cape Breton Island (route 10).

HISTORY BUFFS

Cupids in Newfoundland & Labrador was the site of Canada's first English settlement in 1610 (route 3); Ferryland followed in 1621 (route 2). Long before the English, the Beothuks roamed Newfoundland (route 5), and the Vikings visited L'Anse aux Meadows (route 7).

LITERARY TYPES

See the landscapes that inspired Annie Proulx's *The Shipping News* in Trinity, Newfoundland, and Bernice Morgan's *Random Passage* (both route 4). L. M. Montgomery's *Anne of Green Gables* fans are in for a treat in PEI (route 13).

MUSIC LOVERS

The pubs of St John's, Newfoundland hum with live folk music (route 1), as does much of Cape Breton Island (route 10) and Halifax (route 9). Hear traditional Acadian sounds in La Région Évangéline (route 13).

NATURE LOVERS

Go whale-watching off Bay Bulls (route 2), Twillingate (route 5) or Cape Breton (route 10), or hike the rugged trails of Gros Morne National Park (route 6) and Cape Breton Highlands (route 10). Kayak or canoe the waterways of Kejimkujik National Park (route 11) or the coast of PEI (route 13).

TOP ARCHITECTURE

The multi-coloured mansions of Lunenburg in Nova Scotia (route 11) are known for the distinctive "Lunenburg Bump", while the grand buildings in Saint John, New Brunswick were built after the great fire of 1877 (route 14).

INTRODUCTION

An introduction to Maritimes and Newfoundland's geography, customs and culture, plus illuminating background information on cuisine, history and what to do when you're there.

Dramatic coastline, Green Gardens, Gros Morne National Park

EXPLORE MARITIMES & NEWFOUNDLAND

Snow-capped mountains, mesmerizing fjords, dense forests and the freshest seafood in the world. Canada's four Atlantic provinces are bound by their natural beauty and seafaring traditions, yet each has its own rich cultural identity.

Atlantic Canada is perhaps one of the most startlingly beautiful regions of Canada. Here are the achingly lonely beaches of Nova Scotia, the distinctive sense of humour and charming friendliness of the people of Newfoundland and Labrador, the old-world, Prince Edward Island farmers, and the graceful elegance of New Brunswick's towns. The French and British fought over the three Maritime provinces for almost two hundred years, and today the French-speaking Acadian population remains culturally distinct. After the American Revolution, Loyalists flooded Atlantic Canada, adding another cultural layer. Newfoundland and Labrador's early history was dominated by the seasonal cod, whale and seal fisheries, with year-round "outports" eventually settled by hardy English and Irish fishermen giving the province much of its character today.

Covid-19 Updates

In early 2020, Covid-19 swept across the globe, being categorized as a pandemic by the World Health Organization in March 2020. While travelling in Canada, be sure to heed all local laws, travel advice and hygiene measures; flouting these means risking your own health but can also put a strain on local communities and their medical infrastructure. While we've done all we can to make sure this guide is accurate and up to date, permanent closures and changed opening hours are likely in the wake of coronavirus, so be sure to check ahead.

GEOGRAPHY AND LAYOUT

The area covered in this book is vast, some half a million square kilometres, much of it isolated wilderness fronting Canada's eastern Atlantic coast. The ocean, and especially the Bay of Fundy and Gulf of St Lawrence, dominates life here, with the port of Halifax in Nova Scotia the region's biggest city. The tours in this book begin with the port of St John's, then proceed geographically across Newfoundland and Labrador from east to west, taking in the most popular and attraction-rich areas of the province. The focus then shifts to Nova Scotia, Prince Edward Island, and

Boats docked at fishing village near Cavendish, Prince Edward Island

finally New Brunswick.

You'll need a car to make the most out of the area, as public transport is limited to a handful of long-distance bus lines and railway routes. Most cities are small enough to explore on foot, though local taxis are usually easy to find.

HISTORY

It is thought Vikings visited the region, calling it 'Vinland', in around AD 1000, though they didn't stay long and had little impact – the Beothuk and Mi'kmaq peoples who had lived here for centuries were only displaced by later waves of European arrivals (although many communities still live on reserves. Italian John Cabot, sailing under the English flag, explored the region in the 1490s, with fishermen from France, Spain and England exploiting the vast stocks of cod here soon after. In the Maritimes, the French settled what became known as 'Acadie' in Nova Scotia in the 17th century, and gradually spread throughout the region. In the 18th century the Acadians were expelled from their villages and many went on to form 'Cajun' communities in Louisiana. Some returned and rebuilt, forming the Acadian

DON'T LEAVE THE MARITIMES AND NEWFOUNDLAND WITHOUT...

Visiting Fogo Island. Weathered fishing huts, traditional outports, a community of artists and one of the world's most exclusive hotels occupy one of the most beautifully preserved islands in the region. See page 47.

Driving the Cabot Trail. Atlantic Canada's most scenic highway cuts across the searing coastal headlands and plunging forested valleys of Cape Breton Island. See page 71.

Sampling a lobster supper. It's hard to resist the all-you-can-eat mussels, scallops, chowder and fresh lobster suppers served up on Prince Edward Island. See page 93.

Experiencing live folk music in St John's. The historic pubs of Newfoundland and Labrador's capital jump with the sounds of local fiddle players, singers, accordions, mandolins and guitars most nights. See page 27.

Taking an iceberg- and whale-watching trip. Whale-watching is big business all over Atlantic Canada in the summer, but an added attraction at ports like Twillingate in Newfoundland are towering icebergs. See page 49.

Experiencing Acadian culture. One of Canada's most resilient cultures – distinct French heritage, tasty cuisine, and vibrant music – is alive and well in PEI and New Brunswick. See page 92.

Driving the Fundy Trail Parkway. Explore this rugged and mesmerizing section of the Bay of Fundy coast, with swirling waters, fresh lobster and the highest tides in the world. See page 100.

Spending the night at Battle Harbour. This evocative and isolated 18th-century fishing village off the coast of southern Labrador, accessible only by boat, is a truly a magical place. See page 64.

Iceberg off the coast of Labrador

community of today – almost 33 percent of New Brunswick is French-speaking, and it is Canada's only officially bilingual province. An influx of American Loyalists in 1783 bolstered British settlements in New Brunswick and Nova Scotia, and the region flourished thereafter, principally through logging, fishing and shipbuilding.

CLIMATE

Because of the Gulf Stream, the coastal areas of Atlantic Canada experience a relatively mild climate, despite their latitude. In July average temperatures range 14–23°C in Halifax and Charlottetown, 13–25°C in Fredericton, and 11–22°C in Saint John. However, in winter, inland temperatures can be especially low in New Brunswick and on Cape Breton Island. The weather in Newfoundland and Labrador can vary even more dramatically, with relatively mild summers on the coast, but a year-round polar and sub-Arctic climate in mainland Labrador. Average July temperatures range 11–20°C in St John's and 10–19°C on Fogo Island. Though winter sports are popular all over Atlantic Canada, most attractions, hotels and restaurants outside of the cities open only during the summer months (June to September), when the weather is at its warmest.

POPULATION

The population of Atlantic Canada is a little under 2.5 million. Newfoundland and Labrador has a population of just over half a million (with just 5 percent living in Labrador).

LOCAL CUSTOMS

Atlantic Canada follows much the same cultural traditions of the rest of the country, though there are some local quirks and idiosyncrasies. Kitchen parties are a big part of life in Newfoundland, impromptu get-togethers of family and friends that often end up with singing, guitar playing and a beer or two. Acadian culture, most prominent in New Brunswick, will seem familiar to that of Quebec, though there are some differences in French accent and culinary traditions.

POLITICS AND ECONOMICS

Since 2020, the premier of Newfoundland and Labrador has been Andrew Furey of

Indigenous Maritimes

This travel guide describes places that include the traditional lands and Treaty territories of many Indigenous Peoples, including the Mi'kmaq. Travelling offers us the privilege of being a guest among our hosts and building relationships with them. As you travel, take the opportunity to learn the history of a place; support Indigenous businesses and artists; and make connections with the people who continue to inhabit these lands.

Georgian house, Nova Scotia   *Cabot Trail, Cape Breton*

the Liberal Party. The 2021 provincial election confirmed Furey as premier. The Liberal Party is also in power in Nova Scotia, with Iain Rankin as premier. Progressive Conservative Dennis King is Premier of Prince Edward Island. Agriculture, tourism, and the fishery dominate PEI's small but dynamic economy, with an especially large annual potato crop. However, the aerospace, information technology and bioscience sectors are also growing. The current Premier of New Brunswick is Progressive Conservative Blaine Higgs. New Brunswick's economy is indelibly linked to its neighbour the USA, with much of its booming petroleum, seafood and pulp and paper sectors dependent on exports. Today, Atlantic Canada is one of the world's most enticing destinations, boasting empty roads and gorgeous scenery.

TOP TIPS FOR VISITING THE MARITIMES AND NEWFOUNDLAND

Make reservations. It's crucial to make reservations for accommodation (especially in Newfoundland and Labrador), Lighthouse Picnics, and whale-watching trips.

Bears. Black bears are present throughout Newfoundland and Labrador, Nova Scotia and New Brunswick (but not in PEI). Hikers need to be aware of them, but attacks are very rare. If a black bear approaches you, speak calmly and firmly, avoid eye contact, and back away slowly. Never run or try to climb a tree. If the bear begins to follow you, drop something (not food) to distract it. If the bear attacks, fight back and make lots of noise. Do not "play dead". Polar bears are also present in Labrador, and should be given a very wide berth.

Unpredictable weather. Even in the summer, weather in Atlantic Canada (especially Cape Breton and Newfoundland) can be extremely changeable. Dress in layers while hiking, regardless of the season. Always wear sunscreen, even in cold weather.

Tourism websites. All four provinces have excellent tourism departments with extremely useful websites: New Brunswick (https://tourismnewbrunswick.ca); Newfoundland and Labrador (www.newfoundlandlabrador.com); Nova Scotia (www.novascotia.com); and Prince Edward Island (www.tourismpei.com).

Provincial holidays. Schools and most businesses are closed on these days in Newfoundland and Labrador: nearest Monday to March 17 (St Patrick's Day); third Mon in April (St George's Day); third Mon in June (formerly "Discovery Day"); and third Mon in July (Orangeman's Day) in; there's also New Brunswick Day (first Mon in Aug) in NB.

Time zones. All of Newfoundland, as well as the Labrador coastal communities south of Cartwright (from L'Anse-au-Claire, on the Québec border, to Norman Bay), is on Newfoundland Standard Time (3hr 30min behind GMT, and 1hr 30min ahead of Eastern Standard Time). Most of Labrador (Cartwright, Happy Valley-Goose Bay and Labrador West), as well as the Maritime Provinces, is on Atlantic Time, half-an-hour behind Newfoundland time and 1hr ahead of Eastern Standard Time.

Lobster

FOOD AND DRINK

Lobsters, scallops, mussels and salmon: seafood reigns supreme in Atlantic Canada. Restaurants and pubs source ingredients from small-batch producers, local farmers and fishermen, as well as a growing number of excellent craft breweries.

While lobster shacks, seafood restaurants and fish and chip shops are genuinely magnificent in the Maritimes and Newfoundland and Labrador, there's a lot more to discover. Cities such as Halifax, St John's and Charlottetown have their own multicultural restaurant scenes, as well as a number of highly-rated gourmet restaurants. There's "donairs" in Nova Scotia, Lebanese food in PEI, French-influenced Acadian dishes in New Brunswick and caribou and moose burgers in Newfoundland and Labrador. It's a fascinating scene; in the same rural community you might have a local diner serving Irish stew and fried cod, a high-end bistro offering local, seasonal menus and craft beers, and a *Tim Horton's* coffee shop open at 6am at the local gas station.

LOCAL CUISINE

Cuisine across the four provinces is similar, but there are some local differences and specialities worth seeking out.

Newfoundland and Labrador
Newfoundland's staple food has traditionally been cod fish, usually in the form of fish and chips, though with sup-

plies dwindling, this has become more of a luxury. More common are salmon, haddock, halibut and hake, supplemented by more bizarre dishes like "cod tongues" (actually the meat in the fish cheek), "jiggs dinner" (salted beef and vegetables), fish and brewis (salt cod with hard bread, softened by pork fat and molasses) and seal flipper pie. It's possible (given the province's regulations) but rare for restaurants to serve fresh moose and caribou, though many islanders join in the annual licensed shoot and, if you befriend a hunter, you may end up across the table from a hunk of either animal. Caribou meat from Labrador is far more common, often turning up in burgers, and local bakeapples (cloudberries), blueberries and partridgeberries (loganberries) are used in jams, desserts, pies and sauces everywhere.

Prince Edward Island
PEI has a well-deserved reputation for cuisine; the island is home to organic farms, fine oysters (Malpeques), softshell clams, cultured mussels and artisan producers of all kinds, from potato vodka and gouda cheese, to ice cream and home-made pickles. It remains best

Oysters and mussels   *Fiddleheads*

known for the excellence of its lobsters, which are trapped during May and June and again in late August and September; the catch is kept fresh in saltwater tanks to supply the peak tourist season (this careful management is one of the reasons the lobster population is flourishing). "Lobster suppers" are great value on the island, where you'll get mountains of seafood for around $40.

Nova Scotia

Nova Scotia is especially famous for its blueberries, Annapolis Valley apple pie and "fat archies" (a Cape Breton molasses cookie). The port town of Digby is celebrated for its scallops and its smoked herring or "Digby chicks". In the 19th century, Irish and Scottish immigrants introduced oatcakes and shortbread to Cape Breton Island, along with traditional stews and Scottish-style smoked salmon. Nova Scotia also has its own lobster fishery, with lobster shacks and lobster suppers common on Cape Breton Island.

New Brunswick and Acadian cuisine

New Brunswick is known for its fiddleheads (fern shoots) and dulse (edible seaweed) from Grand Manan Island, as well as its fresh Bay of Fundy and Gulf of St Lawrence lobsters. The largest Acadian population in the Maritimes also influences the food of the province. Acadian cuisine is similar but not exactly the same to that of Québec, with *galettes* (oatmeal and molasses cookies), *ploye* (buckwheat pancakes), *fayots au lard* (pork

and beans), and *poutines* (delectable fruit pastries, not to be confused with the *poutine* of Québec). Rappie pie (or "râpure", from *patates râpées*, "grated potatoes" in French) is an especially tasty Acadian dish of meat or fish and potatoes.

WHERE TO EAT

While you'll find a huge variety of restaurants in Halifax (and to a lesser extent in St John's, Moncton, Saint John and Fredericton), serving international cuisines, the relatively small populations scattered through the Atlantic provinces means smaller towns and villages often feature just one or two restaurants, especially in Newfoundland and Labrador. Local diners often cook up a range

---

The Halifax "donair"

What is the Halifax "donair", and why does it have (sort of) cult status? The donair is much like a typical doner kebab, but uses fresh, lean ground beef (instead of lamb) and a slightly sweet milk-based garlic sauce instead of the usual tzatziki. Legend has it that it was created in a small tavern in Greece, and introduced to Canada in 1973. Today you can order donair pizza and donair subs in addition to the original – hard to believe, but Nova Scotian expats often experience severe homesickness for this eastern Mediterranean delight. King of Donair (see page 114) is said to have initiated the craze in the 1970s.

Outdoor dining at a restaurant in Halifax

of standard dishes, from fried chicken to pasta and burgers, but seafood dominates most menus.

Pubs

Even in the cities, pubs are great places to eat in all four provinces, often doubling as restaurants (and live music venues) as much as drinking holes. Traditional Maritime and Newfoundland cuisine – Irish stew, cod and chips, lobster rolls – often accompany pub standards like tacos, burgers and sandwiches on menus, and the quality is often very good, especially when it comes to seafood. Note that "taprooms" attached to local craft breweries are quite different, often serving only basic snacks or no food at all.

Fish and Chip shops

Newfoundland and Labrador is sprinkled with locally celebrated fish and chip shops, some of them no more than shacks on the side of the road – North Street Cafe in Brigus (see page 40) is a good option.

Lobster shacks and suppers

No-frills lobster shacks selling fresh, live lobsters, as well as freshly boiled lobsters are common throughout the Maritimes. Usually there will be somewhere outside to sit and enjoy the cooked lobsters, though tools (essential) are not always provided; sellers will often crack the shells for you in that case. Self-caterers will be able to boil their own lobsters – a fairly simple though harrowing

process for some – though the biggest problem will be finding a pot big enough. Another tradition in Prince Edward Island and on Cape Breton Island is the "lobster supper", usually a set menu anchored around a main serving of fresh lobster, eaten on long communal tables in local halls or restaurants.

Chain restaurants

All the usual fast-food suspects and chains are present in Atlantic Canada. Local chains include Prince Edward Island-based Cows Creamery ice cream parlours (www.cowscreamery.ca), Nova Scotia's King of Donair (see page 114), Newfoundland's Mary Brown's (https://marybrowns.com), and New Brunswick's Pizza Delight (www.pizzadelight.com) and Greco Pizza (https://greco.ca).

Food hall and markets

Food halls and markets crammed with places to eat as well as fresh food stalls are fun places to eat in the Maritimes, usually home to local vendors selling regional snacks and produce. In Nova Scotia, Halifax Seaport Farmers' Market features over 250 vendors (see page 69), while the Halifax Brewery Farmers' Market opens Wednesdays and Saturdays (www.halifaxbrewerymarket.com). The small university town of Wolfville over in the Annapolis Valley also hosts an excellent Farmers' Market (www.wolfvillefarmersmarket.ca). In New Brunswick, Saint John's City Market (see page 97) is a favourite place for lunch, while

Beer at a brewery in New Brunswick

Charlottetown features the relatively new Founders' Hall Market (see page 87) and it's own farmer's market (https://charlottetownfarmersmarket.com) every Saturday. Don't miss Fredericton, which is home to one of Canada's Top 10 Community Markets.

DRINKS

Beer is the tipple of choice in Atlantic Canada, with a growing number of craft brewers competing with the big brands. Rum, reflecting the region's old seafaring connections with the Caribbean, is also a popular drink. The region's British and Irish roots are also reflected in a relatively high number of tearooms – where tea is always served with milk.

Beer
The huge explosion of craft or micro-brewed beers in North America over the last few decades has hit the Maritimes in a big way. In New Brunswick there's Flying Boats Brewing (see page 119) and Graystone Brewing, while Nova Scotia has Annapolis Brewing (see page 118) and Propeller (www.drinkpropeller.ca) among many others. In PEI, there's Copper Bottom Brewing (see page 118). Newfoundland and Labrador has Quidi Vidi Brewery (http://quidividibrewery.ca) and RagnaRöck (see page 58).

Spirits
Newfoundland Screech is a blended dark rum popular all over the region. Iceberg Vodka really is made with water harvested from Newfoundland icebergs, while Crystal Head Vodka (sold in the skull-shaped bottles) is also produced in Newfoundland. Ironworks Distillery in Nova Scotia (see page 80) and Myriad View Artisan Distillery (https://straitshine.com) in PEI produce high quality rums, vodka, gin and brandy. New Brunswick also has a number of very good distilleries, including Moonshine Creek in Waterville and Fils du Roy in Caraquet.

Wine
The Annapolis Valley in Nova Scotia is Canada's up-and-coming wine destination – its vineyards knock out some surprisingly decent vintages (see https://winesofnovascotia.ca). Newfoundland specializes in various berry-based wines, with producers such as Auk Island (see page 50); PEI has its own small scene, led by producers such as Rossignol Estate (www.rossignolwinery.com); and New Brunswick has a number of excellent wineries (www.winesofcanada.com/nb.html).

Food and Drink Prices
Throughout this book, price guide for a two-course meal for one with an alcoholic drink:
$$$$ = over $75
$$$ = $51–75
$$ = $25–50
$ = below $25

The Carleton in Halifax

ENTERTAINMENT

Atlantic Canada has more pubs per head than just about anywhere else on the planet, and with a rich legacy of British and Irish folk music, you can listen to live bands most days of the week.

Nightlife in the Maritimes and Newfoundland and Labrador principally revolves around pubs, many of them historic establishments but often just local watering holes as full of regulars as tourists. Live music is as important as the food and drink in these places, and the quality of local folk, rock and alternative bands throughout the region is extremely high. In the summer live theatre is also popular, in the form of local or travelling shows, festivals or dinner theatres – the latter usually highlight local cultural traditions and come with a slap-up supper.

68). Nova Scotia's (and the region's) oldest pub is the Fo'c'sle (http://focsle chester.com) in Chester, open, astonishingly since 1764. Even small towns and villages usually have a pub – tiny Torbay in Newfoundland boasts the oldest pub on the island, Mrs. Liddy's, which operates as much as a community centre as a bar. The newer breed of craft brewery tap rooms that have spread across the region are a little different, though they often feature live music too; the focus is on quality beers more than anything else, and food is rarely served.

PUBS

The pubs of Atlantic Canada are friendly, lively places that serve up not only the usual tipples, but great food and live music. St John's and Halifax contain the most drinking holes, but all the big cities contain numerous examples, often with historic roots going back to the British colonial period. Many have a strong Irish component, like Erin's Pub (see page 119), Olde Dublin Pub (see page 120) and Old Triangle Irish Alehouse (see page

LIVE MUSIC

Live music (often local or Irish folk music) performed in pubs or in special venues is a big part of life in Atlantic Canada. Newfoundland and Labrador and Cape Breton Island (see page 74) are best known for more traditional folk music, but all four provinces boast high-quality live bands and performers, many with a national or global following. There's fiddler Natalie MacMaster from Cape Breton, folk pop singer Jenn Grant and rocker Rich Aucoin from Hal-

Gros Morne Theatre Festival, Cow Head

ifax, The Flummies from Labrador, and The Once from St John's, among many, many others. Much live music takes place inside pubs, small intimate venues where as long as you are eating and drinking, you'll be entertained for free. The bigger cities feature purpose-built venues such as The Carleton (see page 119) in Halifax, where there's usually a small charge for performances.

THEATRE

Theatre is thriving in Atlantic Canada, with all the major cities featuring performances venues, and smaller towns and rural areas often hosting summer-only festivals and performances, from Shakespeare to shows highlighting local culture. The largest professional theatre company in the region is the Neptune Theatre in Halifax (see page 121), while the Confederation Centre of the Arts in Charlottetown, PEI (see page 121) is best known for its annual production of the *Anne of Green Gables* musical. Theatre New Brunswick is based at the Fredericton Playhouse, while the Imperial Theatre (www.imperialtheatre.ca) in Saint John hosts a wide range of performances, as does the French-English bilingual Capitol Theatre in Moncton (https://capitol.nb.ca/en). St John's in Newfoundland contains several venues, from the Holy Heart Theatre (https://holyheart theatre.com) to The Majestic at 390 Duckworth Street.

These are complimented by smaller regional theatres such as the Chester Playhouse (see page 120) in Nova Scotia, Woody Point Heritage Theatre (see page 53) in Newfoundland, and the Victoria Playhouse in PEI (see page 90). "Dinner Theatre", which includes a show (usually a comedy) and a meal is also popular here, with the Grafton Street Dinner Theatre in Halifax (see page 121), Water Street Dinner Theatre (see page 98) in Saint John, and the Feast Dinner Theatres (https://feast dinnertheatres.com) in PEI.

Local theatre/cultural performance
The region's dinner theatres often highlight Atlantic Canada, but there are several places where the focus is always on local dialects, idiosyncrasies and culture. The Spirit of Newfoundland (see page 121) celebrates the music and comedy of Newfoundland and Labrador, as do the performances of Theatre Newfoundland Labrador at the Gros Morne Theatre Festival in Cow Head (see page 55), the Rising Tide Theatre (www.risingtidetheatre.com) in Trinity, and the Grand Bank Regional Theatre (www.grandbanktheatrenl.com). In New Brunswick, Le Pays de la Sagouine (https://sagouine.com) hosts Acadian performances throughout the summer (as does the Théâtre populaire d'Acadie; https://tpacadie.ca), while Cape Breton Island is home to numerous shows, festivals and performances celebrating its Scottish and Celtic heritage (see page 74).

Hikers on the Avalon coast

OUTDOOR ACTIVITIES

With vast swathes of untouched forest, rugged mountains, wild rivers and a massive coastline, outdoor adventure is easy to find in Atlantic Canada, with hiking, sailing, kayaking, and fishing in some of the most beautiful surroundings in the world.

Atlantic Canada's mountains, lakes, rivers and forests offer the opportunity to indulge in a vast range of outdoor pursuits, from rock climbing to zip-lining. The most popular activities are fishing, hiking, kayaking and whale-watching, much of this taking place in the region's spectacular national parks, of which there are 10 altogether. In terms of spectator sports, the only major North American franchise here is the Halifax Thunderbirds of the National Lacrosse League (NLL), but there are several other professional sports teams playing in Canadian national or regional leagues.

OUTDOOR ACTIVITIES

Atlantic Canada's national parks are prime targets for outdoor activities, especially hiking, camping and kayaking.

Hiking

Atlantic Canada boasts some of the nation's finest hiking. All of the national and many provincial parks have well-marked and well-maintained trails, and a visit to any park centre or local tourist office will furnish you with adequate maps of the local trails. One of the most rewarding hikes is the 35km, three-day backcountry camping and hiking adventure from the eastern end of Western Brook Pond in Gros Morne National Park. Cape Breton Highlands National Park (see page 74) in Nova Scotia features 26 hiking trails signposted from the Cabot Trail.

Long-distance hiking trails

Many of the long-distance trails in the region form part of the Trans Canada Trail (https://thegreattrail.ca). Negotiating much of the length of the Avalon Peninsula in Newfoundland, the East Coast Trail (www.eastcoasttrail.com) passes through fishing communities, provincial parks, national historic sites and a couple of ecological reserves. The core 336km section stretches from Topsail Beach to Cappahayden, with six designated, non-serviced campsites on route.

Over in Nova Scotia, the Celtic Shores Coast Trail (www.celticshores.ca), runs for 92km from Port Hastings to Inverness on the west coast of Cape Breton Island. On Prince Edward Island, the 449km Confederation Trail system (www.tourismpei.com/pei-confederation-trail) weaves its way

Kayaking in New Brunswick   *Whale watching off Newfoundland*

across the bucolic heart of the island from east to west. In New Brunswick the 57.75km Dobson Trail (http://fundy hikingtrails.com) runs from Riverview to Fundy National Park.

Cycling

Beyond the cities, the region's relatively empty roads are ideal for cyclists. Dedicated routes include the Newfoundland T'Railway Provincial Park, an 880km bike-packing rail trail that crosses Newfoundland from east to west. The Robinson's Island Trail System in Prince Edward Island National Park (see page 90) is another popular destination for mountain bikers, as is Kouchibouguac National Park, which boasts 60km of some of the best (and level) trails in Canada.

WATER SPORTS AND ACTIVITIES

Atlantic Canada is one big water playground, with yachting, canoeing and whale-watching incredibly popular.

Canoeing and Kayaking

The easiest way to explore the Kejimkujik National Park (see page 80) and its flat-water rivers and lakes is by canoe. You can also rent canoes or kayaks at Kouchibouguac National Park, but one of the most popular kayaking trips in New Brunswick is at the Hopewell Rocks (see page 103). Bonne Bay in Newfoundland's Gros Morne National Park is another excellent if breezy location for kayaking (see page 53).

Whale-watching

Humpback whales, fin whales, right whales, minke whales, long-finned pilot whales and even beluga and orcas can be seen in the region's clear waters over the summer months. Places such as St Anthony and Bull's Bay in Newfoundland, St Andrews in New Brunswick, and Cape North, Digby Neck and Pleasant Bay in Nova Scotia are known for their high-quality operators.

SPECTATOR SPORTS

Atlantic Canada is as hockey mad as the rest of the country. The Halifax Mooseheads (www.halifaxmooseheads. ca) play in the Quebec Major Junior Hockey League. The Acadie–Bathurst Titan (http://letitan.com), Cape Breton Eagles (https://capebretoneagles. com), Charlottetown Islanders (https:// charlottetownislanders.com), Moncton Wildcats (https://moncton-wildcats. com) and Saint John Sea Dogs (https:// sjseadogs.com) also play in the league.

The Halifax Thunderbirds (www. halifaxthunderbirds.com) play in the National Lacrosse League (NLL), while the Halifax Hurricanes (www.halifax hurricanes.ca) play in the National Basketball League of Canada, as do Charlottetown's Island Storm (http://storm basketball.ca), Moncton Magic (https:// monctonmagic.ca) and St. John's Edge (https://sjnbl.prestosports.com/land ing/index).

BEST ROUTES

Walking around St John's

ST JOHN'S WALK/A STROLL AROUND ST JOHN'S

The capital of Newfoundland and Labrador, St John's provides the best introduction to island life, not least for the province's top museum, The Rooms, its historic cathedrals, enticing restaurants, friendly pubs and a flourishing live music scene.

DISTANCE: 5km
TIME: A full day
START: Harbourside Park
END: Signal Hill (Cabot Tower)
POINTS TO NOTE: As with the rest of Newfoundland and Labrador, most sights in St John's are only open fully in the summer months (June to September); if you're planning to visit any the museums or historic sites, avoid doing this walk Monday to Wednesday, even in summer, as sights are often closed on these days. The tour can be completed on foot, but the last section up Signal Hill is quite strenuous (the tour is too tough for young children on foot): if legs are tiring, take a taxi (Newfound Cabs; tel: 709-744 4444, www.newfoundcabs.com), or use The Link (late June to late Sept Wed–Sun; $10 for day pass), which will hopefully be running again in the summer of 2022 (download the map and schedule at www.metrobus.com/thelink/about.html). Ongoing COVID-19 restrictions may impact the opening times listed below – check websites to confirm.

For centuries life in St John's has focused on its harbour, a dramatic jaw-shaped inlet approached through the 200m-wide channel of The Narrows. French, English, Basque and Portuguese fishermen set up seasonal camps here in the early 16th century, and though Sir Humphrey Gilbert claimed the area for England in 1583, a permanent settlement wasn't established until well into the 1600s. In its heyday, the port was crammed with ships from a score of nations; today, although traffic is not as brisk, it draws a mixed maritime bag of trawlers, container ships and oil construction barges (since the collapse of the cod fishery in the 1990s, offshore oil exploration has taken off).

St John's still boasts a lively nightlife, but the rough houses of the waterfront have been replaced by shops, slick office buildings and chic restaurants, and its inhabitants – of whom there are about 200,000 – are less likely to be seafarers than white-collar workers, artists and students. Yet the waterfront remains the social hub,

View over town from The Rooms

sprinkled with traditional pubs that showcase the best of Newfoundland and Labrador folk music – one good reason for visiting in itself – as well as providing the backdrop for hit TV show *Republic of Doyle*.

WATER STREET

Water Street has always been the commercial heart of St John's, still lined with former mid-19th-century mercantile buildings. Most of these buildings were erected after the Great Fire of 1846. Today it's crammed with souvenir shops, modern office blocks, cafes and bars that many different visitors can enjoy Tiny **Harbourside Park ❶**, on Water Street, is the logical place to start a visit to the city: it was here – or at least hereabouts – that Sir Humphrey Gilbert landed in 1583 to claim the island for England. You can take in a series of historical plaques in the park that gives all the background. Behind the park are two bronze dogs, a Newfoundland and a Labrador. The **Newfoundland National War Memorial** stands on the other side of the street.

Stroll southwest along Water Street into the heart of town, taking in the wonderful scene, and turn right when you reach the Romanesque Revival **St John's Court House ❷** at 194 Water St, completed in 1904 – the stone staircase here leads up to Duckworth Street.

Folk Music in St John's

St John's nightlife revolves around its traditional pubs on Water Street and adjoining George Street – it's not hard to believe there are more watering holes per square kilometre here than any other city in Canada. Boisterous but always friendly, these are the best spots to hear Newfoundland folk music, a distinctive style that evolved from the fiddles and button accordions brought over by the first English and Irish settlers (you'll also hear more generic Celtic or Irish folk music here). "Folk Night at the Ship" (265 Duckworth St; Wed 9pm; $5) draws a decent crowd, while Erin's Pub (186 Water St), Bridie Molloy's (www.bridiemolloys.ca), and Kelly's Pub (25 George St) among many others, all host live music (George Street between Water Street and Adelaide Street is most lively strip).

At some point you're likely to be invited to be "screeched in", a touristy but fun ritual for all newcomers (basically anyone not from St John's) – routines vary, but it usually involves kissing a stuffed cod, reading something written in Newfoundland slang, and downing the local brand of Screech Rum. The best of the island's dozen folk festivals, the Newfoundland and Labrador Folk Festival (https://nlfolk.com), is held in Bannerman Park in St John's in early August.

ANGLICAN CATHEDRAL OF ST JOHN THE BAPTIST

Perched on the hillside, just above Duckworth Street, is the blue stone **Anglican Cathedral of St John the Baptist** ❸ (16 Church Hill; www.ourcathedral.ca; Mon–Fri 9am–4pm), with the main entrance on Gower Street on the north side (if it's locked ask at the office off Church Hill). The cathedral was designed in Gothic Revival style by the English architect Sir George Gilbert Scott. Begun in 1847, much of the church burnt down in 1892, but Scott's son rebuilt it to the original plans. As you exit the cathedral, Gower Street to the northeast is lined with the famous candy-coloured clapboard houses common all over the city – collectively dubbed "**Jellybean Row**". As you walk uphill along Cathedral Street you'll pass another bright example of the style on Bond Street. Keep walking up steep Garrison Hill to Harvey Road.

BASILICA-CATHEDRAL OF ST JOHN THE BAPTIST

On the other side of Harvey Road lies the grandest of the city's churches, the twin-towered **Basilica-Cathedral**

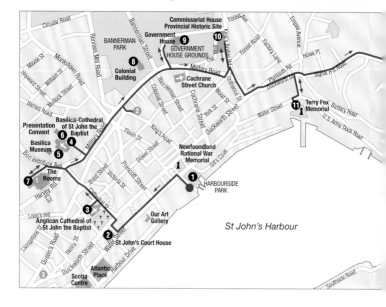

Far left is the Anglican Cathedral then St Andrews Church, The Rooms and then the Basilica

of St John the Baptist ❹ (https://
thebasilica.church; Mon–Fri and
Sun 8am–4pm, Sat 9am–5pm). The
Romanesque cathedral was completed in 1855, with the interior featuring 65 stained glass windows
illuminating a delightfully ornate and
embossed gold, maroon and deep-
green ceiling.

Next to the cathedral, in what used to
be the old Bishop's Palace, the **Basilica Museum** ❺ (usually open early
June to Aug Tue–Fri 9am–noon and
12.30–4pm; $2) includes the Mullock
Episcopal Library completed in 1860,
with many of its ancient tomes still on
display. Panels explain the history of the
Basilica and the Library, enhanced with
old vestments, reliquaries and religious
artefacts.

It's also worth trying to visit the
Presentation Convent ❻ (June–Sept
Mon–Fri and Sun 1–4pm, Sat 10am–
4pm; Oct–May Mon–Fri 1–3pm; free)
on the other side of the cathedral,
home of the revered, marble **Veiled
Virgin** statue, carved in Rome by
sculptor Giovanni Strazza and deliv-
ered here in 1856. It's a stunning work
of art, the marble creases perfectly
mimicking a silk veil delicately draped
across Mary's face.

THE ROOMS

On the other side of Bonaventure
Avenue from the cathedral is **The
Rooms** ❼ (9 Bonaventure Ave; www.
therooms.ca; June–mid-Oct Mon–Sat
10am–5pm; Wed till 9pm; Sun noon–
5pm; mid-Oct to May closed Mon;
$10), holding Newfoundland and Lab-
rador's best historical, ethnographic
and fine art collections.

The fascinating permanent exhibit
chronicles the island's history beginning
with its earliest inhabitants, the Maritime Archaic Peoples, and their succes-
sors, the Dorset Inuit and the Beothuks.
You should also aim to grab lunch here,
at **The Rooms Café** (see ❶). This excellent spot also offers awe-inspiring views
of the city and shouldn't be missed during your visit.

Map

200 m / 220 yds

N

❶❷ Johnson
Geo Centre

Georges Pond

Signal Hill

Signal Hill Road

P

❶❸ Signal Hill
Visitor Centre

Newfoundland
Chocolate Company

Signal Hill
National Historic
Site

P

❶❹ Cabot Tower

The Narrows

Government House

COMMISSARIAT HOUSE PROVINCIAL HISTORIC SITE

From The Rooms it's a relatively easy (downhill) 1.3km-stroll along Military Road to Commissariat House, but it's worth a small detour at Kings Street (at the junction known as "Rawlin's Cross") to grab a dessert at **Moo Moo's Ice Cream** (see ②). The life-size statue of a little girl nearby (aka "Spencer Girl") commemorates the old Bishop Spencer College. Beyond Rawlin's Cross you'll pass Bannerman Park and the stately **Colonial Building** ⑧, which once served as Newfoundland and Labrador's legislature (1850–1959), and **Government House** ⑨, the residence of the Lieutenant-Governor of Newfoundland and Labrador since 1831 (free tours are available Mon–Fri 9am–4pm by appointment only). The handsome **Commissariat House Provincial Historic Site** ⑩ (11 King's Bridge Rd, at Military Rd; usually open late May to early Oct Wed–Sun 9.30am–5pm; $6) itself was completed in 1820 as the home and offices of the assistant commissary general, who was responsible for keeping the British garrison in St John's paid, fed and clothed. Its rooms have been restored in authentic period style.

SIGNAL HILL NATIONAL HISTORIC SITE

It's just over 1km to the first attractions on **Signal Hill**, a huge, grass-covered hunk of rock with sensational views and lots of history. To avoid the hike up look for "The Link" bus stop just outside Commissariat House on Kings Bridge Road, or around the corner at St Thomas Church – the bus zips right up Signal Hill via the Johnson Geo Centre. If you're walking, you can detour en route to the **Terry Fox Memorial** ⑪ on Water Street, marking the spot where the beloved cancer activist began his legendary "Marathon of Hope" in 1980.

Johnson Geo Centre

The **Johnson Geo Centre** ⑫ (175 Signal Hill Rd; www.geocentre.ca; Apr–June and Sept–Dec Wed–Sun 10am–4pm; July and Aug daily 10am–4pm; $12) is devoted to earth sciences, with interactive family-friendly exhibits on the Earth, Newfoundland and Labrador's geology, and the complex relationship between the Earth and human beings. Special exhibits also focus on the corals and sponges of Atlantic Canada, and oil and gas exploration.

Signal Hill Visitor Centre

A little further up Signal Hill Road lies **Signal Hill Visitor Centre** ⑬ (http://pc.gc.ca/signalhill; usually open May to early Sept daily 10am–6pm; early Sept to mid-Oct Wed–Sun 10am–6pm; $3.90), whose well-chosen displays and dramatic 20-minute multimedia presentation explore the military and civilian history of the site, particularly the bitter struggle for the city between

Cannon on Siganl Hill   *Cabot Tower*

France and England in the 18th century. There's also a **Newfoundland Chocolate Company** café (www.newfoundlandchocolatecompany.com). Rearing up above The Narrows from here, **Signal Hill National Historic Site** (open access) is laced with hiking trails, taking in various remnants of old gun batteries and the grounds of the **Signal Hill Tattoo**, held here in July and August (signalhilltattoo.org) – the last performance is usually at 3pm.

Cabot Tower

End your tour on the panoramic summit of Signal Hill. It's crowned by **Cabot Tower** ⑭, a short and stout stone structure completed in 1900 to commemorate John Cabot's voyage of 1497 and Queen Victoria's Diamond Jubilee. The tower contains the Signal Hill Heritage Shop (open Apr–Nov), and outside in the car park there's a plaque honouring Guglielmo Marconi, who confirmed the reception of the first transatlantic radio signal here in December 1901. If it's still light, the walk back into town from here is very pleasant, where you can end the day with dinner at fabulous **Chinched** (see ③), followed by some live music on George Street.

Food and Drink

① THE ROOMS CAFÉ

9 Bonaventure Ave; www.therooms.ca/café; tel: 709-757 8097; Mon–Sat 10am–4pm, Sun 11am–5pm (mid-Oct to May closed Mon); $$

Set on Level 4 of the city's premier museum, with fabulous views of the city and harbour below, this contemporary restaurant focuses on Newfoundland and Labrador's food heritage. Think rich seafood chowders, traditional salt cod cakes and panko-crusted cod tacos.

② MOO MOO'S ICE CREAM

88 Kings Rd; tel: 709-753 3046; June–Sept Mon–Thu noon–6pm, Fri–Sun noon–10pm; Oct–May limited hours, but always open Fri–Sun noon–6pm; $

This beloved ice-cream counter inside The Market convenience store serves sorbets and luscious ice cream with local flavours like partridgeberry (loganberry) and bakeapple (cloudberry), plus pies, cakes and cookies.

③ CHINCHED

5 Bates Hill; tel: 709-722 3100; www.chinched.com; Tue–Fri 11am–2pm and 5.30–10pm, Sat 5.30–10pm; $$$

Superbly crafted cuisine from chefs/owners Shaun Hussey and Michelle LeBlanc – sandwiches made with artisanal meats, amazing cheese and charcuterie boards and local mussels, potato-wrapped cod and crispy pig ears. Reservations recommended.

Cape Spear Lighthouse

THE IRISH LOOP

Traversing the southeastern arm of the jagged Avalon Peninsula, this three-day road-trip snakes from one enticing rock-bound cove to another, taking in the island's early Irish history, whale-watching, puffin colonies, wild caribou and ancient fossils.

DISTANCE: 375km return

TIME: 2 or 3 days

START/END: St John's

POINTS TO NOTE: This tour is designed as a road-trip – cars are easy to rent in St John's. It's recommended in summer; most of the sights on this route close completely or partially from September to May, though the roads themselves are usually open year-round. It can be completed in two or three days (for accommodation, see page 106), and is easily combined with the other tours around the Avalon (Baccalieu Trail, see page 37). It's important to make some reservations in advance; it's also best to reserve whale- and bird-watching tours from Bay Bulls, and the Mistaken Point tour, as well as tickets for the Southern Shore Folk Arts Dinner Theatre.

St John's sits on the northeast corner of the Avalon Peninsula, a roughly rectangular slab of land divided into four arms. The Irish Loop – a combination of highways 10, 90 and 1 – is named for the Irish history dominating the southeastern arm, which goes back to the early 17th century – many locals retain a distinct Irish brogue even today. On route are some of Newfoundland's most popular attractions: panoramic Cape Spear, the historic remains and lighthouse picnics at Ferryland, the whales and puffins of Witless Bay, and the fossils of Mistaken Point.

CAPE SPEAR

From St John's it's a 15km drive via Rte-11 to **Cape Spear National Historic Site ❶** (www.pc.gc.ca/en/lhn-nhs/nl/spear; open access), a rocky, windblown headland that is nearer to Europe than any other part of mainland North America. The cape is criss-crossed by boardwalks, the most obvious of which leads up from the car park past the Heritage Shop, CCG Alumni Association Art Gallery and the modern lighthouse to the squat and

Whale in Bay Bulls	*Puffins and Razorbills in Witless Bay*

rectangular Victorian **Cape Spear Lighthouse** (mid-May to mid-Oct daily 10.30am–5.30pm; $3.90), the oldest in the province.

In the spring and early summer, the waters off the cape are a great place to spy blue-tinged icebergs, and there's a fairly reasonable chance of spotting whales.

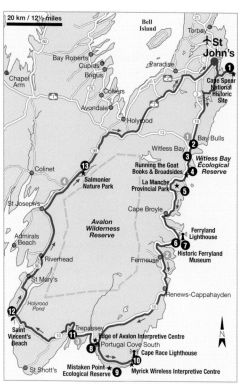

BAY BULLS AND WITLESS BAY

From Cape Spear it's around 35km south to the village of **Bay Bulls ❷**, where boats depart for the tiny off-shore islets comprising the **Witless Bay Ecological Reserve**. The best time to visit is between mid-June and mid-July, when over 800,000 birds gather here – the reserve has the largest **puffin colony** in eastern Canada and there are also thousands of storm petrels, common murres, kitti-wakes, razorbills, guille-mots and cormorants. In addition, the area is home to the largest population of **humpback whales** in the world, and finback and minke whales are often spotted between June and August. Most boat trips run for two hours (book in advance): try Gatherall's (90 Northside Rd, Bay Bulls; https://gatheralls.com) or O'Brien's Boat Tours (Lower Rd; www.obriensboattours.com). Grab lunch at the excellent **PondHouse Eatery** (see ❶), a short drive further south along Rte-10.

River of Boats

ON TO FERRYLAND

After lunch, be sure to stop at the **River of Boats** ❸, some 7km south of Bay Bulls on Rte-10 (you'll see the tiny sails on the pond on the right side of the road). Local Max Morgan handmade these miniature boats, along with fishing scenes and model lighthouses – he usually has them out on the pond from late May to early September (free but donations appreciated).

From here it's another 6km south to Tors Cove, the home of **Running the Goat Books & Broadsides** ❹ (50 Cove Rd Tors Cove; https://runningthegoat.com; June–Sept Sat and Sun 10am–5pm or by appointment), just off the main highway. This old-fashioned print shop and publisher is a great spot for Newfoundland souvenirs (art, handmade books and original prints). From Tors Cove its 11km on Rte-10 to the turning for beautiful **La Manche Provincial Park** ❺ (mid-May to mid-Sept; $10 per vehicle), ideal for hikers; La Manche Falls Trail and La Manche Village Trail (which takes in the famous suspension bridge at the now abandoned village) both take around one hour each to complete. From the park entrance it's a leisurely 21km drive down to the village of **Ferryland** ❻, where you can stay at **Dunne's Bed & Breakfast** (see page 106). Try and reserve tickets to the **Southern Shore Folk Arts**

Dinner Theatre (www.ssfac.com/dinner-theatre), which operates June to September and combines typical Newfoundland fare with live music.

FERRYLAND

Begin day two with a leisurely tour of **Ferryland**, an early English colony created by George Calvert, the first Baron Baltimore. Calvert dispatched a band of prospective colonists under Captain Edward Wynne to what is now Ferryland in 1621 (Baltimore himself only stayed here briefly 1628 to 1629). Ferryland was totally destroyed by the French in 1696; the ruins of the first colony were rediscovered only in 1980. Today the site is preserved as the fascinating **Colony of Avalon** (http://colonyofavalon.ca; mid-June to mid-Sept daily 10am–6pm; $16). Start at the Visitor Centre, which adds context through panels, videos and some of the artefacts actually found here, from grape seeds to cannon balls. You can also visit the **Historic Ferryland Museum** (late June to early Sept Mon–Sat 10am–4pm, Sun 1–4pm; $3) a bit further up the road, set in wooden premises built in 1916 for the Bank of Montreal and crammed with historic artefacts.

Lighthouse Picnics

Lighthouse Picnics ❼ (http://lighthousepicnics.ca; late May to Sept Wed–Sun 11.30am–4.30pm; from

Mistaken Point Ecological Reserve Fossil Bed

$28; reservation required) sells fabulous picnic lunches at the lighthouse on Ferryland Head (2km on dirt roads from the Colony of Avalon). Find a spot on the headland and enjoy the fabulous views while you eat (getting there involves a 25-minute walk from the parking lot, each way). If you'd rather take the tour at Mistaken Point, skip the picnic and make sure you leave Ferryland by noon at the latest – you can grab an earlier lunch/snack at **Tetley Tea Room By The Sea** (see ❷).

MISTAKEN POINT ECOLOGICAL RESERVE

From Ferryland, continue south on Rte-10 for another 59km to the **Edge of Avalon Interpretive Centre** ❽ (http://edgeofavalon.ca; mid-May to late Oct daily 10am–6pm; $5; tours at 1pm; $20), which lies just off the road in Portugal Cove South. The center provides an introduction to the **Mistaken Point Ecological Reserve** ❾ (some 16km further along a gravel road), a UNESCO World Heritage Site home to over 6,000 incredibly well-preserved Precambrian fossil remains in situ. Discovered in 1969, it is considered one of the most important fossil sites in the world (the fossils range from 575 to 542 million years old), but what makes it particularly special is that visitors are free to clamber all over the rocks. Visitors can only visit the site on an official tour (by minibus and then on foot; book ahead) – allow three-and-a-half-hours altogether.

Cape Race

If you're not able to take the Mistaken Point tour (or have time afterwards), you can drive along the same gravel road all the way to Cape Race, 21km from the Edge of Avalon Interpretive Centre. The isolated 32m-high **Cape Race Lighthouse** ❿, built in 1907 (interior closed to the public), lies atop a jagged headland above the Atlantic – it's been a maritime landmark for centuries. Learn more at the adjacent **Myrick Wireless Interpretive Centre** (June–Aug daily 11am–5.30pm; Sept 1 to mid-Sept Fri–Mon noon–5.30pm; $10, includes Edge of Avalon Interpretive Centre), a replica of the Marconi Marine Radio Station built here in 1904 (famous for receiving the Titanic distress call in 1912).

TREPASSEY

From Cape Race it's around 150km (2hr 30min) drive back to St John's the way you came, or 200km to complete the Irish Loop (around 3hr) –just about doable in daylight in the summer, but far more enjoyable if you take another day. The **Edge of the Avalon Inn** (see page 107) is in the old fishing village of **Trepassey** ⓫, 32km from Cape Race on Rte-10. The **Inn restaurant** (see ❸), is also a good place for dinner.

Salmonier Nature Park

SALMONIER LINE

Day three begins with an initial 33-km drive across wild moorland to **Holyrood Pond**, where Rte-10 becomes Rte-90, aka the "Salmonier Line" (after the Salmonier River). The road drops down to **St Vincent's Beach ⑫**, a narrow isthmus between the ocean and the Pond. Because of a steep drop-off close to the shore, it's often possible to spy whales very close to the beach.

From St Vincent's it's a beautiful, winding 69km drive to **Salmonier Nature Park ⑬** (June to early Sept daily 10am–6pm; free). Stop for lunch at **Riverview Lounge & Restaurant** (see **④**), 12km short of the park. The park itself features a 3km boardwalk trail through forest and wetlands, passing enclosures where injured native animals are rehabilitated.

From here it's around 66km (45min to 1hr) drive back to St John's.

Food and Drink

❶ PONDHOUSE EATERY

1 Island Cove Road, Bay Bulls; www.facebook.com/pondhouseeatery; tel: 709-334 2786; Mon–Fri noon–8pm, Sat and Sun 9am–8pm; $$

Friendly diner overlooking the beautiful Maggoty Cove Pond above Bay Bulls, serving a large menu from hot turkey sandwiches and fish tacos to hefty burgers, pizza and fish and chips.

❷ TETLEY TEA ROOM BY THE SEA

15–25 Pool Rd, Ferryland; www.ssfac.com; tel: 709-432 2052; late June to mid-Sept Fri–Tue 11am–4pm; $$

Good value, home-cooked food, from sandwiches to classic Newfoundland dishes like "fish n' brewis"; salt fish served with hard bread, scrunchions (salt pork rinds) and fried onions. Order with big blue pots of Tetley Tea.

❸ EDGE OF THE AVALON INN RESTAURANT

111 Coarse Hill Road, Trepassey; www.edgeoftheavaloninn.com; tel: 709-438 2934; usually open late May to late Sept daily for breakfast, lunch and dinner; $$$

The refined dining room at this small inn serves traditional Newfoundland cod fish cakes and fish and chips, and cod tongue dinners, as well as pastas and roast chicken – there's also a dedicated kids' menu.

❹ RIVERVIEW LOUNGE & RESTAURANT

Rte-90, St Catherine's; tel: 709-521 2210; Late May to Aug daily noon–8pm, Sept–late Nov Wed–Sun noon–8pm, late Nov to late May Fri–Sun noon–8pm; $$

Conveniently located on the Salmonier Line, with a pub-style menu that covers all the usual from fish and chips to traditional "jigs" dinners. The bar and lounge tends to open longer hours.

Brigus

THE BACCALIEU TRAIL

*Looping around the wild and lesser-visited Bay de Verde Peninsula,
the Baccalieu Trail takes in some of Newfoundland's oldest villages and
some its most pristine scenery, from the lovely beach at Salmon Cove to
the rocky headlands of Bay de Verde town and Grates Cove.*

DISTANCE: 560km return
TIME: 3 days
START/END: St John's
POINTS TO NOTE: This tour is designed as a road-trip from St John's, where cars are easy to rent. As with the rest of Newfoundland and Labrador, most sights on the Baccalieu Trail are only open fully in the summer months (June to September). Though the tour begins and ends in St John's, it is easily combined with the other routes around the Avalon (Irish Loop, see page 32) – the Baccalieu Trail just from Brigus to Dildo is 378km. It's important to reserve accommodation (see page 107) far in advance, as there's not a lot of choice.

The Baccalieu Trail (primarily highways 80 and 70) covers the northwestern section of the Avalon Peninsula (this section is known locally as the Bay de Verde Peninsula), starting with Brigus and historic Cupids at the southern end of Conception Bay, one of the oldest European settlements in North America. The trail is named after Baccalieu Island at the peninsula's northern tip, (derived from the Portuguese or Spanish words for codfish), one of the world's greatest seabird nesting sites. Nearby Grates Cove at the end of the road contains a real surprise and culinary treat in the form of Grates Cove Studios. The western side of the peninsula runs along the wild shores of Trinity Bay, taking in the absorbing boat museum in Winterton, historic Cable Station at Heart's Content and the beautiful fishing port of Dildo.

BRIGUS

From St John's it's just over an hour's drive (85km) to **Brigus ❶**, a prosperous seafaring town on Conception Bay, and the gateway to the Bay de Verde Peninsula. The chief sight here is **Hawthorne Cottage National Historic Site** (1 South St; www.pc.gc.ca/en/lhn-nhs/nl/hawthorne; usually open June to early Sept; check website for latest times; $3.90), once the home of Captain Robert Bartlett (1875–1946). Built in 1830 in the romantic "picturesque" style (rare in

Cupids Legacy Centre

Newfoundland and Labrador), his home is adorned with a trellised, wrought-iron, wraparound veranda, while the tiny rooms (a bit like ship cabins) have been atmospherically preserved and crammed with family belongings. History buffs should try to visit the nearby **Ye Olde Stone Barn Museum** (4 Magistrates Hill; www.brigusheritage.ca; June to early Sept Fri–Sun 9am–5pm), which chronicles the history of Brigus. Grab a quick and tasty lunch at the **North Street Café** (see ❶), before moving on.

CUPIDS

Tiny **Cupids** ❷, 3km north of Brigus, was the unlikely site of Canada's first English settlement. Today it's a pretty village straggled along the shore of Cupids Cove and dominated by the jagged cliffs of Spectacle Head on the other side. The absorbing **Cupids Legacy Centre** (368 Seaforest Drive; https://cupidslegacycentre.ca; early June to early Oct daily 9.30am–5pm; $8.65; $14.75 with the Plantation) chronicles the history of the site. Just down the road, at the location of the original English colony, **Cupids Cove Plantation Provin-** **cial Historic Site** (467 Seaforest Drive; www.seethesites.ca/the-sites/cupids-cove-plantation.html; mid-May to early Oct daily 9.30am–5pm; $6; $14.75 with Legacy Centre) is a site you can wander on your own, but you'll get more out of it by taking a guided tour (30min; included with entry). Spend the night at **Cupids Haven B&B** (see page 107), which also serves supper, and try to get tickets to a Shakespeare performance at the outdoor **Perchance Theatre** (www.perchance theatre.com) on the hotel grounds.

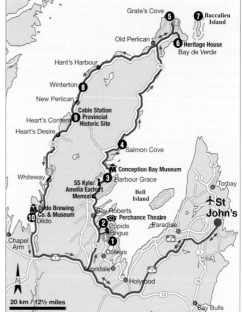

Bay de Verde   *Salmon Cove*

HARBOUR GRACE

From Cupids it's a winding 30km drive along Rte-70 to **Harbour Grace ❸**, another historic town spread out for 4km along Water Street. As you enter the town look for the statue and memorial (an original DC-3 aircraft) to **Amelia Earhart**, the first woman to cross the Atlantic by plane solo – she took off from Harbour Grace in 1932. Out in the harbour opposite the memorial is the hulk of the **SS Kyle**, a 1913 steamship that ran aground here and has been in elegant decay since 1967. Further along Water Street stands the **Conception Bay Museum** (late May to mid-Sept Mon–Fri 10am–noon and 1–4pm, Sat noon–4pm; $3), which has displays on Easton, Earhart, and the fishery in Harbour Grace.

SALMON COVE

Continue north on Rte-70 for around 17km to the small fishing village of **Salmon Cove**, where **Salmon Cove Sands ❹** is one of the most enticing beaches in Newfoundland (there's a small charge of around $2.50 for entry). If it's sunny, the wide stretch of smooth grey sand is a great spot for a picnic; buy supplies at Foodland (on route at 8 Goff Ave, Carbonear).

GRATES COVE AND AROUND

Leave time for the 60km drive north on Rte-70 from Salmon Cove to the sce-nic tip of the peninsula at **Grates Cove ❺**. On the way stop in at the beautiful port town of **Bay de Verde ❻** and the **Heritage House** (7 Blundon Point; www.baydeverde.com; June to Aug daily 10am–4pm) to learn about **Baccalieu Island ❼**, home to the largest colony of storm-petrels in the world. Grates Cove itself feels like the edge of the world, with rugged hiking trails, historic rock walls and stunning views of the Atlantic Ocean (often speckled with icebergs). Spend the night at **Grates Cove Studio** (for accommodation see page 107), check out the art and sample the exquisite Syrian-Cajun-Newfoundland cuisine of owners Terrence and Courtney Howell in the **Open Studio Restaurant** (see ❷).

WINTERTON

Begin day three with a 48km drive south from Grates Cove (via Rte-70 and Rte-80) to **Winterton**, home of the **Wooden Boat Museum of Newfoundland & Labrador ❽** (http://woodenboatmuseum.com; early June to late Sept daily 10am–5pm; $8). Here skilled craftsmen preserve traditional boat-building techniques in a special workshop at the back. The surprisingly large museum itself tells the story of the wooden boat from Inuit kayaks to modern punts and dorys.

HEART'S CONTENT

Continue south 12km on Rte-80 to **Heart's Content**, a small town with an

Wooden Boat Museum of Newfoundland and Labrador

Food and Drink

1 NORTH STREET CAFÉ

30–32 North St, Brigus; tel: 709-528 1350; daily 10am–5pm; $$

Beloved local diner, with a shaded outdoor deck, serving freshly made sandwiches and classic Newfoundland dishes: moose stew, pan-fried cod, saltfish cakes and seafood chowder with shrimp and sea scallops.

2 OPEN STUDIO RESTAURANT

Main Rd, Grates Cove; www.gratescove studios.ca; tel: 709-587 3880; May–Oct Thu–Tue 1–8pm; $$$

The restaurant at Grates Cove Studios is one of the island's culinary gems, with dishes utilizing local seafood, berries, mushrooms and other foraged ingredients. The menus might include anything from Cajun/Creole dishes (snow crab *etouffee*), to Korean and Syrian-influenced food. They also do boxed lunches.

3 BROWN'S RESTAURANT

445 Trinity Rd (Rte-80), Whiteway; http://brownsrestaurant.ca; tel: 709-588 7829; Fri–Sun noon–7.30pm; $$

Friendly spot overlooking Trinity Bay and Whiteway's Shag Rocks, offering excellent cod, salmon, shrimp, roast turkey and roast beef dinners, all sorts of chicken options and decent Angus steaks. Save room for the homemade desserts (including local blueberry and partridgeberry pies).

important history. In 1858, the **Cable Station Provincial Historic Site** 9 (on Rte-80 in the centre of town; late May to early Oct daily 9.30am–5pm; $6) was the scene of the audacious attempt to connect North America with Britain by telegraph cable. It was eight years before an improved version, running from Valentia in Ireland, was successfully laid by Brunel's *Great Eastern* – the cable revolutionized communications, and Heart's Content became an important relay station to New York, a role it performed until technological advances made it obsolete in the 1960s. The site preserves the old cable operating room from 1918, with all the archaic equipment in pristine condition, as well as videos and displays chronicling the history of the venture. There's not a lot of choice when it comes to eating on this side of the peninsula – aim to have lunch at **Brown's** (see 3), another 26km south of Heart's Content on Rte-80.

DILDO

Continue south another 19km to Dildo 10 (no one really knows where the name comes from). The Dildo Brewing Co. & Museum (1 Front Rd; http://dildo brewingco.com; Sun–Thu 11am–7pm, Fri and Sat 11am–8pm) comprises the absorbing Dildo Outport Heritage Museum (open summer only), and a fine craft brewery. It's a straightforward 100km drive (via Rte-80 and the Trans-Canada Highway) back to St John's (just over one hour).

Trinity

THE BONAVISTA PENINSULA

The Bonavista Peninsula pokes out into the ocean for some 120km, its shredded shoreline confettied with beautiful bays, coves and islands. This two-day route takes in picturesque fishing ports, restored fishing villages, puffin colonies, rugged hiking trails and isolated lighthouses.

DISTANCE: 165km
TIME: 2 days
START: Clarenville (Trans-Canada Highway)
END: Cape Bonavista
POINTS TO NOTE: This tour is designed as a road-trip. Though the tour begins at Clarenville on the Trans-Canada Highway (190km or two hours drive from St John's), it is easily combined with other routes around the Avalon Peninsula (Irish Loop, see page 32; Baccalieu Trail, see page 37), or with the Kittiwake Coast tour further north (see page 45). It's important to reserve accommodation (see page 107) far in advance, as there's not a lot of choice; we recommended also booking tickets for the Rising Tide Theatre, and for dinners at the Twine Loft, in advance. As with the rest of Newfoundland and Labrador, most sights on the Bonavista are only open fully in the summer months (June to September).

Fishermen from the West Country of England began using the coves of the Bonavista Peninsula as summer stations for the migratory cod fishery as early as the 1570s. The English – led by merchants from Poole – settled on the Bonavista in numbers during the 17th century and established one administrative centre, Trinity. Today Trinity remains one of the biggest draws in the region, with a fine collection of old buildings serving as museums and atmospheric rental homes. Cape Bonavista itself remains a wild, isolated promontory, with the nearby town of Bonavista offering a smattering of historic attractions.

TRINITY AND AROUND

From the Trans-Canada Highway at Clarenville it's around 70km (1hr drive) to history **Trinity ❶**, one of Newfoundland's most attractive towns – it served as the prime location for 2001 film *The Shipping News*. Founded in the 17th century, the settlement's narrow lanes are edged by a delightful ensemble of white and pastel-painted clapboard houses, all set between a ring of hills and the deep and intricate Trinity Bay.

The architectural high point of the village is **St Paul's Anglican Church**, completed in 1894, whose perfectly proportioned Gothic Revival exterior is adorned by elaborate scrollwork.

Trinity Provincial Historic Sites

Make for the **Trinity Visitor Centre** (mid-May to early Oct daily 9.30am–5pm; $6 for all three sites, $20 with Trinity Historical Society sites) on West Street, with general exhibits and information about the town's history and the surrounding area. Buy tickets here for two more Trinity Provincial Historic Sites, plus the independently managed Trinity Historical Society sites (see below).

Trinity Historical Society sites

The **Trinity Historical Societ**y (www. trinityhistoricalsociety.com; mid-May to mid-Oct daily 9.30am–5pm; combined admission ticket $20, includes Provincial sites) manages four more historic sites in the village. Opposite the church is the modest but entertaining **Trinity Museum**, a classic saltbox home from the 1880s. The **Green Family Forge** on the corner of West Street and Dandy Lane displays artefacts associated with the blacksmiths of Trinity between 1750 and 1955. The nearby **Lester-Garland House** on West Street is a three-storey Georgian-style brick home with expertly reproduced period rooms. Finally, the

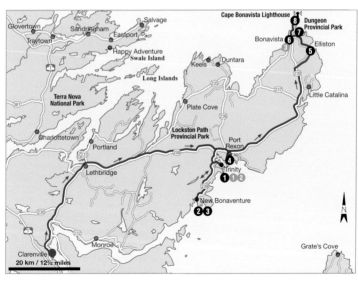

Trinity Bay with lighthousse from Skerwink Trail

reconstructed **Cooperage** is living history museum where you can see a traditional cooper (barrel maker) at work. Have lunch with a view at **Dock Marina Restaurant** (see ❶).

New Bonaventure
More history is on offer at **New Bonaventure ❷**, about 15km southwest of Trinity on Rte-239. A side road pushes on – fork right over the hill as you descend into the village and continue for another 500m until you reach St John's Anglican Church at the end of the road. A gravel road leads 600m down from here to the **Random Passage Site ❸** (www.random passagesite.com; late May to late Sept daily 9.30am–5.30pm; $10), a replica, early 19th-century outport with fishing stages, roughly hewn wooden shacks, a church and a school. The location is stunning, but the authentic mud and stone hovels emphasize the harsh nature of life here, and how everything revolved around the fishery.

Skerwink Trail
Hikers might prefer to drive 10km northeast to **Port Rexton**, where the **Skerwink Trail ❹** is a 5.3-km loop featuring sensational views of sea stacks, whales, icebergs, kittiwakes, gannets, and great black-backed gulls. The trailhead is clearly marked off Rocky Hill Road, south of the main village. Allow around two to three hours.

Back in Trinity spend the night at the **Artisan Inn** (see page 107), and book a table at the **Twine Loft** (see ❷), for dinner. Be sure to check out the performances at **Rising Tide Theatre** (www.risingtidetheatre.com), which include **New Founde Lande Trinity Pageant**, a walking tour of the town led by actors.

CAPE BONAVISTA AND AROUND

Begin day two with a 52km drive on Rte-230 from Trinity to Bonavista, right up at the northern tip of the peninsula. On route take a short detour (Rte-238) to the small village of **Elliston ❺**, with around 135 hobbit-like cellars for storing produce through the winter dug into the hillside (you can visit some of them). The village also boasts the closest viewing of puffins from land in North America, a colony of over 80,000 spread over the cliffs.

Bonavista
The history of **Bonavista ❻** is explored at the **Ryan Premises National Historic Site** (10 Ryan's Hill Rd; www.pc.gc.ca/en/lhn-nhs/nl/ryan; June to early Sept Wed–Sun 10am–6pm; $3.90), a 19th-century fish-processing complex on the harbour. The nautical heritage of Bonavista is celebrated at the **Ye Matthew Legacy** (15 Roper St; http://thematthew.ca; mid-June to mid-Sept daily 9.30am–5pm; $7.25). The other noteworthy sight in Bonavista is the plain white clapboard **Mockbeggar Plantation Provincial Historic Site** (Roper St; mid-May to early Oct Wed–Sun 9.30am–5pm; $6, includes entry to light-

Dungeon Provincial Park

Food and Drink

① DOCK MARINA RESTAURANT

1 Dock Ln, Trinity; www.dockmarina.
com; tel: 709-464 2133; May–Oct daily
noon–7pm; $$

Waterfront restaurant housed in 300-year
old fishing premises, specializing in seafood
and traditional Newfoundland meals (cod,
snow crab, mussels, shrimp, scallops,
salmon, lobster and fish and chips), as well
as burgers, sandwiches, salads and fried
chicken.

② TWINE LOFT

57 High St, Trinity; www.trinityvacations.
com; tel: 709-464 3377; May–Oct Tue–
Sun 8am–10am and dinner served at
5.30pm and 7.45pm (only at 7pm in May
and Oct); $$$

Exceptional dining experience, in a
beautifully restored fishing shed and
waterside deck. Breakfast is open to non-
guests, but the main event is dinner, where
the restaurant serves set three-course
menus at two sittings in summer.

③ MIFFLIN'S TEA ROOM

21 Church St, Bonavista; https://mifflins-
tea-room.business.site; tel: 709-468
2636; June–Oct daily 8am–9pm; $

Serves afternoon tea, veggie dishes, local
specialities (fish cakes with beans, bacon
wrapped scallops) and outstanding desserts
– everything is made from scratch, so check
the wi-fi (free) while you wait.

house). The house has been returned to
its appearance in 1939. The saltbox Big
Store outside may date from 1733, which
would make it the oldest building on Newfoundland. Have lunch at **Mifflin's Tea
Room** (see ③), in the centre of town.

Dungeon Provincial Park

Drive down Lance Cove Road to **Dungeon Provincial Park ❼**, home to a
locally celebrated sea cave with a natural archway through the rugged cliffs.
Semi-wild horses often graze here. Continue 6km north along Cape Shore Road
to **Cape Bonavista ❽** in the afternoon.

Cape Bonavista

Cape Bonavista itself is a witheringly
beautiful, desolate headland of dark-grey
rock and pounding sea inhabited by hun-
dreds of puffins. Explorer John Cabot is
supposed to have first clapped eyes on
the Americas here in 1497, exclaiming –
or so it's claimed – "O buona vista!" ("O,
happy sight") and, true or not, a statue
has been erected in his honour. Cape
Bonavista is still overseen by the 10m-tall
red-and-white-striped **Cape Bonavista
Lighthouse** (mid-May to early Oct Wed–
Sun 9.30am–5pm; $6, includes entry to
Mockbeggar Plantation) built in 1843,
attractively restored to its appearance
in 1870 when it was occupied by an
80-year-old lighthouse keeper, Jeremiah
White, and his family; costumed guides
give the background and the adjacent
interpretive centre gives an overview of
the island's crucial lighthouse system.

Barbour Living Heritage Village, Newtown

THE KITTIWAKE COAST

Newfoundland and Labrador's Kittiwake Coast embodies everything the province is known for: beautiful, rugged coastline and empty beaches; historical, picturesque outports such as Fogo and Twillingate; and pristine waters speckled with basking whales, dolphins, seabirds, and glittering icebergs.

DISTANCE: 400km
TIME: 3 days
START: Gambo (Trans-Canada Highway)
END: Twillingate
POINTS TO NOTE: This tour is designed as a road-trip, beginning at the Trans-Canada Highway at Gambo (300km from St. John's) and ending at Twillingate, though it's possible to complete a loop by continuing south on Rte-340 back to the Trans-Canada at Notre Dame Provincial Park. It is also easily combined with the Baccalieu Trail. It's important to reserve accommodation (see page 107) far in advance; you must also reserve dinner at Fogo Island Inn Dining Room in advance. As with the rest of Newfoundland and Labrador, most sights on this route are only open fully in the summer months (June to September). Fogo Island is connected to the mainland by a scheduled ferry service (4–5 daily 8.30am–8pm), from the tiny port of Farewell. Times change seasonally, with most departures stopping at the Change Islands along the way.

Studded with wide sandy beaches, the Kittiwake Coast (or the "Straight Shore" as it was traditionally known) encompasses the northern coastline of central Newfoundland, named after the seagull with the distinctive, shrill call. This three-day road-trip incorporates the scenic "Road to the Shore" and the "Road to the Isles", both rich in local history. The Barbour Living Heritage Village in Newtown and the gorgeous outports of Fogo Island evoke Newfoundland's early fishing settlements, while Boyd's Cove features a rare insight into the Beothuk people, the island's original inhabitants. The tour concludes in Twillingate, famed for its whale-watching and towering icebergs that come floating down from Greenland every summer.

NEWTOWN

From the Trans-Canada Highway at Gambo, Rte-320 (aka "Road to the Shore") runs northeast along an increasingly wild Kittiwake Coast. It's some 85km to the charming village of **Newtown ❶**, the "Venice" of Newfoundland,

its clapboard homes and pretty St Luke's Church set on 17 barren, gale-whipped islands linked by bridges. The big attraction here is **Barbour Living Heritage Village** (www.barbour-site.com; late June to early Sept daily 10am–5pm; $10), a collection of clapboard houses, wharves and a tearoom preserved as a living museum – locals dressed in period costume enliven the experience with skits and demonstrations.

LUMSDEN

From Newtown it's just 16km to **Lumsden Beach** ❷, one of Newfoundland's most enticing stretches of sand. It's a great spot for a picnic; buy local snacks,

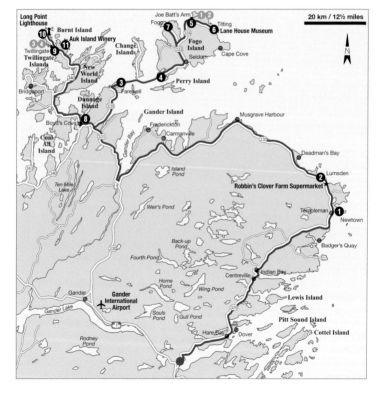

Lumsden Beach

pies and supplies at **Robbin's Clover Farm Supermarket** on the main highway in Lumsden itself. Make sure you leave the beach in time to catch the ferry to Fogo Island – the drive from Lumsden is 125km (allow at least 1hr 30min). In summer the last ferry usually departs at 8pm.

FOGO ISLAND

The "Road to the Shore" continues from Lumsden along the north coast on Rte-330 and Rte-331 – Rte-335 branches off the latter to **Farewell** ❸ and the Fogo car ferry dock (45min sailing time direct, or 1hr 15min via Change Islands). Try to get to the port 1hr before departure to ensure you get on – if it's full you'll have to wait for the next one (no reservations are taken). It's worth buying a museum pass (singe $15, couples $25) if you intend to visit three or more of the 10 local museums (buy the pass at the first museum you visit).

Just 25km long and 14km wide, **Fogo Island** ❹ was first settled by fishermen from the West Country of England. Zita Cobb's Shorefast Foundation (https://shorefast.org) has helped improve infrastructure, and an innovative arts programme (see www.fogoislandarts.ca) has boosted tourism. Yet this has simply highlighted what the locals knew all along – that the air here is cleaner, the ocean saltier, the people friendlier and the scenery more enchanting than anywhere else on the planet.

The best place to stay on the island is the phenomenal **Fogo Island Inn** (see page 107 for a full list of accommodation options), but options in **Joe Batt's Arm** ❺ are often more affordable – the likes of Quintal House lies 27km from the ferry dock on Fogo. Spend all of day two exploring Fogo Island by car, although going by foot allows you to soak up the picturesque surroundings just as much. Note that all 10 of the historic sights on the island feature the same hours and admission (www.townoffogoisland.ca; June–Sept daily 10am–6pm; $5).

Tilting

Visit in the early morning, and you may not want to leave the bewitching village of **Tilting** ❻, some 9km east of Joe Batt's Arm. Gorgeous clapboard cottages, saltboxes, creaky wharves and boathouses cling to the rocks around the placid harbour. The village is proud of its Irish heritage, and the best way to soak it up is to just wander the streets; highlights include the 1890s **Dwyer Premises**, a traditional home and fish processing station; **Lane House Museum**, a saltbox-style home built in 1830; and the tiny **Old Post Office** of 1908. If the sun is out, you should also make a stop at nearby **Sandy Cove Beach**, one of Newfoundland's best stretches of sand.

Joe Batt's Point

Head back to **Joe Batt's Arm** where the **Joe Batt's Point Walking Trail** (4.6km

Tilting

return) snakes along the bay, passing the stylish **Long Studio** and ending at the **Great Auk statue** at the point itself – both fruits of Cobb's innovative arts program. Visit **Brett House Museum** (Brown's Point Rd), built on the other side of the harbour in the early 1870s, and artfully restored in period style. Grab lunch nearby at **Scoff** (see ❶).

FOGO

In the afternoon drive to the town of **Fogo** ❼ (16km from Joe Batt's Arm). It's an extremely picturesque place, surrounded by rocky hills and containing several historic churches. Nearby is craggy **Brimstone Head**, renowned locally for the dubious distinction of being proclaimed one of the "four corners of the world" by the now defunct Flat Earth Society – it's a chilling, nerve-tingling spot regardless, with an easy trail to the 90m summit for the best views on the island.

There are several historic sites in and around the town worth exploring, beginning with **Experience Fogo** (5–7 North Shore Rd), a small but atmospheric collection of wooden buildings preserved to give a sense of the town's fishing heritage: a trap store, stable, carpenter's store and a fish flake leading out to a fishing stage on the harbour.

Just outside the town, the **Marconi Wireless Interpretation Centre** (15 Pickett's Rd Extension) commemorates Marconi's presence here between 1912 and 1931 (the views are worth the drive up alone). Back in Joe Batt's Arm, it's worth splurging on a sensational dinner at the **Dining Room** (see ❷), at the Fogo Island Inn.

There are also a range of walking and hiking routes to choose from in Fogo; there are rolling hills, rocky outcrops and sunset vistas to soak up. Pack up a picnic and head out on an embracing walk around the likes of Brimstone Head, Deep Bay and more.

BOYD'S COVE

Get an early start on day three to catch the first ferry back across to Newfoundland. From Farewell ferry dock it's 29km to the fascinating **Beothuk Site Interpretive Centre** ❽ in Boyd's Cove (Off Hwy-340; mid-May to early Oct daily 9.30am–5pm; $6). The centre commemorates a small village inhabited by the Indigenous Beothuks between 1650 and 1720 – 11 house pits have been identified, with four excavated so far. Some of the 41,000 artefacts dug up are on display, including iron nails stolen from European fishing stations, ingeniously modified by the Beothuks into arrowheads.

After leaving Boyd's Cove continue north for 42km on Rte-340 (aka "Road to the Isles") to Twillingate, crossing the four causeways that connect Chapel Island, New World Island and Twillingate Island to the mainland.

Fogo Island Inn,

Beothuk Interpretation Centre

TWILLINGATE

The outport of **Twillingate ⑨** is one of the largest towns in central Newfoundland, with over 3,000 inhabitants and a rich history that goes back to the 1700s. Twillingate Island became the year-round headquarters of Poole-based merchant John Slade in 1750, after several decades of use by itinerant French fishermen, who gave the place its original name, "Toulinguet", from an island back home in Brittany. Though it remains an old fishing village at heart, it's far more developed than Fogo Island, with whale-watching and iceburg tours on offer. If you visit the town in September, you'll be able to go berry-picking; thousands of bakeapples (cloudberries), partridgeberries (lingonberries) and blueberries smother the slopes around the town.

In the summer there's also plenty of live entertainment most nights in Twillingate – the **Split Rock Brewing Co** (see ③), serves tasty craft beer and burgers. For Twillingate accommodation, see page 107.

Twillingate Museum

Housed in the old rectory, built in 1915 behind St Peter's Anglican Church, the **Twillingate Museum** (1 St Peter's Church Rd, off Main St; https://tmacs.ca; mid-May to early Oct Fri – Tue 9am – 5pm; free), contains several period rooms crammed with historic bric-a-brac, plus a small display of Maritime Archaic artefacts dug up from the nearby Curtis Site (1500 BC)

and an exhibit dedicated to chanteuse Georgina Stirling (the "Nightingale of the North"), who was born in Twillingate in 1867. Have lunch down the street from the museum at **Annie's** (see ④).

Iceberg-Spotting

Between late May and July, the myriad inlets near Twillingate can ensnare dozens of icebergs as they float down from the Arctic, though in these days of climate change it can be hard to predict their appearance. You won't forget the experience if you do encounter one: tinted in shades of aquamarine and white by reflections from the sea and sun, they seem like otherworldly cathedrals of ice, which stand out brilliantly from the blue-green ocean and, if you're particularly lucky, you might witness the moment when one of them rolls over and breaks apart, accompanied by a tremendous grating and wheezing and then an ear-ringing bang. Several local companies offer iceberg-watching boat tours: Iceberg Quest Pier 52, Main St; https://icebergquest.com. Daily departures at 9.30am, 1pm, and 4pm and 7pm in peak season (2hr; $65). May to Oct.
Twillingate Adventure Tours https://twillingateadventuretours.com. Mid-May to mid-Sept 2 – 3 daily; 2hr; $65.
Twillingate Island Boat Tours (Iceberg Man Tours) 50 Main St; www.icebergtours.ca. Mid-May to Sept daily 9.30am, 1pm and 4pm; 2hr; $65.

Iceberg in front of a rocky island near Twillingate

Long Point Lighthouse

Ideally you'd spend the afternoon on a whale-watching or iceberg-spotting boat trip, but landlubbers still stand a good chance of spotting an iceberg from the bright red and white **Long Point Lighthouse** ❿ (262 Main St, Crow Head; May, June and Sept daily noon–5pm; July and Aug daily 10am–5.30pm; $7). The lighthouse occupies a commanding position on a high rocky cliff at the tip of Twillingate North Island, a short drive from the centre of town. Viewpoints and trails lace the headland if you fancy stretching your legs. The old keeper's cottage, built in 1876, has been turned into a small museum, and is well worth a visit if you have enough time.

Auk Island Winery

Back across on Twillingate South Island, end the day at **Auk Island Winery** ⓫ (29 Durrell; https://aukislandwinery. com; daily 9.30am–6.30pm; Oct–Apr Mon–Fri 10am–4pm), which offers a great introduction to Newfoundland's growing number of eminently drinkable fruit wines, made with local blueberries, partridgeberries, bakeapples, raspberries and crowberries.

Food and Drink

❶ SCOFF

159 Main Rd, Joe Batt's Arm, Fogo Island; https://scoffrestaurant.com; tel: 709-658 3663; late May–Nov Wed–Sat 5.30–9.30pm (longer hours July and Aug); $$

Best diner on the island, with finely crafted local dishes including crab cakes and seafood stew – always ask about local specials.

❷ DINING ROOM AT FOGO ISLAND INN

210 Main Rd, Joe Batt's Arm, Fogo Island; https://fogoislandinn.ca; tel: 709-658 3444; daily for dinner; $$

Gourmet dining in Fogo Island's landmark hotel, with seasonal menus that utilize local ingredients: think cod cheeks with dandelion and burnt onion. Non-guests must reserve by emailing dining@fogoislandinn.ca.

❸ STAGE HEAD PUB (SPLIT ROCK BREWING CO)

119 Main St, Twillingate; www.splitrock brewing.ca; tel: 709-893 2228; late June to Sept Thu–Sun 3–11pm; $$

Twillingate's craft brewpub is a real gem, with an outdoor deck, great pub food and a vast selection of tasty beers, from Black Island Stout to Bluff Head Bitter.

❹ ANNIE'S RESTAURANT

128 Main St, Twillingate; https://annies restaurant.ca; tel: 709-884 5999; late May to late Sept 9am–8pm; $$

Meals with a gorgeous harbour view, with an emphasis on seafood, such as salmon in blueberry sauce.

Road through the park

GROS MORNE NATIONAL PARK

Some of Newfoundland and Labrador's most mesmerizing scenery is contained within Gros Morne National Park (a UNESCO World Heritage Site), its bays, wild beaches, straggling villages and wizened sea stacks with a backcloth of bare-topped, fjord-cut mountains. This three-day tour takes in the highlights.

DISTANCE: 230km
TIME: 3 days
START: Deer Lake
END: Cow Head
POINTS TO NOTE: This tour is designed as a standalone road-trip, beginning on the Trans-Canada Highway at Deer Lake (where there's also an airport) and ending at Cow Head further up the Great Northern Peninsula. It can be easily combined with the Viking Trail (see page 56) which also passes through Gros Morne. It's important to reserve accommodation (see page 108) far in advance; you must also reserve tours with Wild Gros Morne, Gros Morne Adventures and Bontours in advance, especially the Western Brook Pond Fjord Boat Tour. It's also wise to buy tickets to the Gros Morne Theatre Festival ahead of time. As with the rest of Newfoundland and Labrador, most sights on this route are only open fully in the summer months (June to September).

Established as a reserve in 1973, Gros Morne encompasses 1,805 square kilometres of wilderness on Newfoundland's west coast. Its forested slopes are home to thousands of moose, woodland caribou and snowshoe hare, while minke whales regularly feed in the two arms of Bonne Bay, the sub-arctic fjord at the heart of the park. The northern segment of the park encompasses Western Brook Pond, a beautiful freshwater fjord, and the flat-topped Gros Morne (806m) mountain itself. Gros Morne has also attracted its fair share of artists and musicians, highlighted at the Trails, Tales and Tunes festival (www.trailstalestunes.ca) held in Norris Point each May.

DISCOVERY CENTRE

From Deer Lake drive 67km northwest (via Rte-430 and Rte-431) into the southern section of the park, stopping first at the **Discovery Centre** ❶ (www.pc.gc.ca/en/pn-np/nl/grosmorne; mid-May to mid-Oct daily 9am–5pm; free with park entry, $10; Nov to mid-May $7.90) on the

Hiking in Tablelands

edge by **Woody Point** to get the latest information. Interactive exhibits inside examine the area's geology, plant and animal life, with special focus on climate change.

THE TABLELANDS

From the Discovery Centre Rte-431 cuts through the **Tablelands** ❷, a Mars-like landscape of reddish, barren flat-topped rock. At 450 million years old, this is one of the few places on Earth where this mantle pokes above ground. Drive 4.5km to the parking area for relatively easy **Tablelands Trail** (4km return; 1hr), which cuts along the base of the main section into the glacially carved Winter House Brook Canyon. Download the guided tour app for the Tablelands or buy a map at the Discovery Centre. It's another 13km from here to Trout River along Rte-431.

TROUT RIVER

Rte-431 comes to an end at **Trout River** ❸, an atmospheric fishing village founded by settlers from Dorset (in England) in the 1820s. Lobster and crab fishing remain the staples, but you can visit several historic buildings (http://townoftroutriver.com; July–Sept daily 11am–6pm; $10) on the sleepy bayfront (Main St). The **Interpretation Centre** (245–247 Main St) contains historic curios and artefacts, old photos and videos on the village,

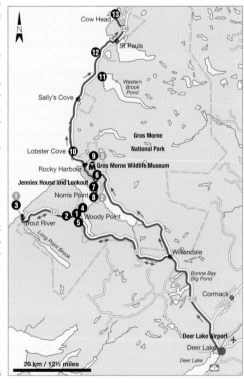

Woody Point   *Bonne Bay from Woody Point Trail*

while the **Jacob A. Crocker Heritage House** (221 Main St) is a picture-perfect yellow saltbox from 1898. While strolling the bayfront stop by the **Seaside Restaurant** (see ❶), for lunch.

WOODY POINT

From Trout River it's 18km back along Rte-431 to **Woody Point** ❹, but it's worth checking in advance to see if **Wild Gros Morne** (https://wildgros morne.com) are running any boat tours this afternoon (they also do sunset cruises). Their zodiac boat tours are a fun way to see Bonne Bay up close (tours depart from **Waters Edge RV Adventure Park** ❺, 3km south from Woody Point on Rte-431).

Woody Point itself is a sleepy fishing village that was once the main port on Bonne Bay. Established by the English fishing merchants Bird & Co around 1800, nothing much survived a devastating fire in 1922, but the clapboard buildings built in subsequent years form an attractive heritage district near the waterfront.

Check out the **Heritage Theatre** in the centre of the village, which hosts an impressive roster of folk musicians and performers throughout the summer, including the **Writers at Woody Point festival** (www.writersatwoodypoint. com) every August. Spend the night at **Bonne Bay Inn** (see page 108).

In terms of walking and hiking trails, Lookout Point is great for bird-watching.

NORRIS POINT

Start day two with a scenic 68km drive around Bonne Bay into the northern section of the national park – you have to backtrack all the way to Wiltonville, then take Rte-430 northeast (allow 1hr). Just before Rocky Harbour, take the left turn to the **Gros Morne Visitor Centre** ❻ (mid-May to late Oct daily 9am–5pm), which has displays on the natural and human history of the park, as well free maps, brochures on hiking trails and details of local boat excursions. Keep driving south from the visitor centre and it's 7km to the thriving community of **Norris Point** ❽ (www.norrispoint.ca), overlooking Bonne Bay where it divides into East and South arms. On the way, stop at **Jenniex House and Lookout** ❼ (late June to mid-Sept daily 9am–7pm; free), a 1926 saltbox home high above the bay. It was moved to this spot in 1995, one of the most jaw-dropping locations in the park. Inside you'll find a craft shop, a small museum of local historic bits and pieces upstairs and a traditional "mug up" – tea and muffins with molasses.

Bonne Bay Marine Station
Right on the waterfront at Norris Point, the **Bonne Bay Marine Station** (1 Clarke's Rd; www.mun.ca/bonnebay; mid-May to early Sept daily 9am–5pm; $9.50), a unit of Memorial University, offers guided tours of its research

Kayakers in the park

facilities and aquarium; tanks feature local lobsters, cod, skate, and even furry sea mouse. **The Cat Stop** (see ❷) next door is a good place for lunch, while **Bontours** (http://bontours.ca) usually operates Bonne Bay cruises from here (June–Sept daily 2pm). Alternatively, **Gros Morne Adventures** (https://grosmorneadventures.com) runs kayak tours and offers kayak rentals from its base nearby at 9 Clarke's Road. On a clear day Bonne Bay serves up some rich sights, with whales, otters, seals and bald eagles sometimes spotted.

ROCKY HARBOUR

Around 10km north of Norris Point (via Pond Road), **Rocky Harbour ❾** is Gros Morne's largest village, curving around a long and sweeping bay with the mountains lurking in the background. Check out the **Gros Morne Wildlife Museum** (76 Main St North; https://grosmornewildlifemuseum.ca; late June to early Sept daily 10am–6pm, may open later; $8). The museum displays over 100 animals in natural scenes: caribou, moose, fox, sea birds, beaver, black bear and even a giant polar bear (the latter was acquired in Nunavut). All the animals were acquired humanely from the Parks Service, found having died naturally or having been killed in accidents before being preserved using modern techniques (not stuffed). Check in to

the bayfront **Ocean View Hotel** (see page 108) tonight and have dinner at nearby **Java Jack's** (see ❸).

LOBSTER COVE HEAD LIGHTHOUSE

Begin your final day with a visit to **Lobster Cove Head Lighthouse ❿** (off Main St North; mid-May to early Oct daily 10am–5.30pm; free with park entry), at the northern end of Rocky Harbour. Completed in 1897, the lighthouse offers stunning panoramas across the bay and a small exhibition on the history of the region.

WESTERN BROOK POND

The remote **Western Brook Pond ⓫**, reached by just one access point, 25km north of Rocky Harbour beside Rte-430, is one of eastern Canada's most enchanting landscapes; 16km of deep, dark-blue water framed by mighty mountains and huge waterfalls. From the parking lot it's a 40-minute (3km) walk on a well-maintained trail through forest and over bog to the edge of the landlocked fjord. When you get to the end, don't skimp on the two-hour boat trip (reservations required; July and Aug daily 10am, 11am, 12.30pm, 1.30pm and 3pm; mid-May to June and Sept to mid-Oct daily 12.30pm; $65; www.bontours.ca). The boat inches its way between the cliffs right to the extreme

Beach at Cow Head

eastern end of the lake, past several huge rockslides, dramatic hanging valleys and former sea caves now marooned high above the water.

BROOM POINT

A further 6km north of Western Brook Pond on Rte-430, **Broom Point** ⑫ (June to mid-Sept daily 10am–5.30pm; free with park entry) is a desolate, windswept promontory crowned with a picturesque smattering of fishing shacks, one of which has been turned into a small fishing museum – guides tell the story of the Mudge family fishing oper-

ation here (1941–75), and also the nearby Paleo-Eskimo site.

COW HEAD

The village of **Cow Head** ⑬, another 11km north of Broom Point on Rte-430, is perched at the most northerly end of Gros Morne National Park. It's best known for its **Gros Morne Theatre Festival** (June to early Sept; http://theatrenewfoundland.com), based at the Warehouse Theatre in the centre of the village. Its programme of drama, music and cabaret is a thoroughly entertaining way to end your visit.

Food and Drink

① SEASIDE RESTAURANT
263 Main St, Trout River; www.seasiderestaurant.ca; tel: 709-451 7381; late May to Sept daily noon–9pm; $$
Freshly caught Newfoundland-style seafood – chowders, lobster, mussels, snow crab, halibut, salmon and cod – served up in a cozy dining room overlooking the Gulf of St. Lawrence. Leave room for the bakeapple cheesecake.

② CAT STOP
2–4 Stones Lane, Norris Point Waterfront; https://bontours.ca/cat-stop; tel: 709-458 3343. June–Sept daily 8.30am–8pm (Fri–Sun till 1am); $

Pub and café with a sun-drenched upper deck, perfect for early drinks and light snacks before or after a kayak or boat trip. Also hosts live folk music in the evenings (Thu–Sun), and has free wi-fi.

③ JAVA JACK'S
88 Main St North, Rocky Harbour; https://javajacks.ca; tel: 709-458 2710; mid-May to early Sept daily 8.30am–8.30pm; $$
Fabulous café and B&B, serving hearty breakfasts (think lobster benny), well-priced lunches (salt cod fish cakes) and dinners such as seared salmon with peach, veggie lasagne and rabbit pie, much of the produce coming from the organic garden.

The Viking Trail

VIKING TRAIL

This route runs along Newfoundland's rugged Great Northern Peninsula, shadowing the Long Range Mountains to some of Canada's best iceberg and whale watching, plus its most extraordinary historic sites – including the only confirmed settlement of 10th century Greenland Vikings on this side of the Atlantic.

DISTANCE: 485km
TIME: 3 days
START: Deer Lake
END: L'Anse aux Meadows
POINTS TO NOTE: This tour is designed as a standalone road-trip, beginning on the Trans-Canada Highway at Deer Lake (where there's also an airport) and ending at L'Anse aux Meadows at the tip of the Great Northern Peninsula. Though it passes through Gros Morne National Park, the park is not covered on this route; it's easy to combine this tour with the more focussed three-day Gros Morne route (see page 51). It's important to reserve all accommodation (see page 108) far in advance, as there's not a lot of choice; it's also best to reserve Northland Discovery Boat Tours in advance, and meals at The Norseman – reservations for boat tours of Western Brook Pond are mandatory. As with the rest of Newfoundland and Labrador, most sights on this route are only open fully in the summer months (June to September).

Stretching between Gros Morne National Park and the township of St Anthony, the Great Northern Peninsula on the western side of Newfoundland is a rugged, sparsely populated finger of land separating the Gulf of St Lawrence from the Atlantic. Its interior is dominated by the spectacular Long Range Mountains, a chain of flat-topped peaks that are some of the oldest on Earth. Rte-430 – aka the Viking Trail – snakes along the western edge of the peninsula, connecting the small fishing villages of the narrow coastal plain. The region's most remarkable sight is the remains of the Norse colony at L'Anse aux Meadows – it's the reason for the "Viking" label. The tip of the peninsula also boasts Newfoundland's longest iceberg-watching season, and is an excellent place to see whales late into the summer.

DEER LAKE TO PORT AU CHOIX

It's a 235km (2hr 30min to 3hr) drive from **Deer Lake ❶** to Port au Choix on Rte-430, mostly traversing a narrow

Western Brook Pond

Interpreter at L'Anse aux Meadows

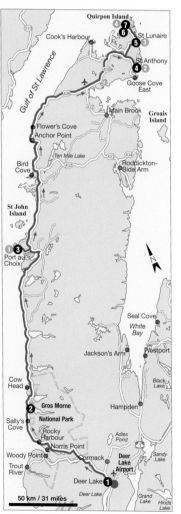

slice of the Great Northern Peninsula between the Gulf of St Lawrence and the Long Range Mountains. The first section of the route cuts through Gros Morne National Park, which deserves special attention (see page 51), but if you have time for just a brief visit consider reserving the first boat trip on **Western Brook Pond ❷** (see page 54), some 96km (just over an hour) from Deer Lake (usually 10am July and Aug).

Port au Choix

Mysterious bone, stone and ivory arte-facts were being discovered by locals in the small fishing village of **Port au Choix ❸** as far back as 1904, but it wasn't until the 1960s that profes-sional archeologists uncovered some astonishing finds: a mass of prehis-toric bones, tools and weapons and several ancient cemeteries, ultimately yielding 117 skeletons from the Neo-lithic period.

This heritage is preserved within the **Port au Choix National Historic Site** (www.pc.gc.ca/en/lhn-nhs/nl/portauchoix; early June to early Sept daily 9am–5pm; $3.90), with a visitor centre set halfway along a bleak head-land 2.5km from the village. Films, touch-screen presentations and arte-facts dug up from Neolithic ceme-teries introduce the various cultures that existed here, while trails lead out across the headland to the sites them-selves. The primary discovery, right in the middle of the village, is a ceme-

The Grenfell Interpretation Centre

tery belonging to the Maritime Archaic Indians, hunter-gatherers who lived here between 3500 and 1200 BC. Have lunch overlooking the harbour at the **Anchor Restaurant** (see ❶), before another long drive through wild upland country to St Anthony on Rte-430 (210km). Check-in for two nights here (Crows Nest Inn, see page 108), after sampling a well-earned craft beer at **RagnaRöck Northern Brewing Co** (http://ragnarockbrewing.com).

ST ANTHONY

Spend day two exploring the remote fishing and supply centre of **St Anthony** ❹, which began life in the 16th century as a seasonal French fishing station (French explorer Jacques Cartier is said to have named it in 1534). It remained French well into the 1800s, when English-speaking Newfoundlanders started to settle the area.

The local **Iceberg Festival** (https://theicebergfestival.ca) begins on the first Friday in June, and today St Anthony remains one of the best places to see icebergs and fin, minke, and orca whales. Book a morning tour with **Northland Discovery Boat Tours** (www.discovernorthland.com), which runs 2hr cruises (mid-May to late Sept; 1–3 daily; from $65). On land, the best place to view icebergs (and have lunch) is **Fishing Point** at the head of the harbour, where there's small lighthouse and **Fishing Point Emporium**

(June–Oct daily 9am–9pm; free) selling local arts and crafts, Labradorite (an iridescent feldspar mineral) and bakeapple ice cream, and has a small exhibition of local flora and fauna. From here you can climb the steep path to the viewing deck at Fishing Point Head, and eat at **Lightkeepers Café** (see ❷).

Grenfell Historic Properties

Devote the afternoon to St Anthony's primary land-based attraction, a group of memorials collectively dubbed the **Grenfell Historic Properties** (www.grenfell-properties.com; July–Sept daily 8am–5pm; Oct–June interpretation centre only Mon–Fri 8am–5pm; combined admission $10), dedicated to the pioneering missionary doctor, Sir Wilfred Grenfell. An Englishman who first came here on behalf of the Royal National Mission to Deep Sea Fishermen in 1892, Grenfell established the region's first proper hospitals, nursing stations, schools and co-operative stores.

Start at the **Grenfell Interpretation Centre** (and excellent handicrafts store) on Maravel Road, which introduces the subject with a film and two floors on Grenfell's life and times, before moving on to the **Grenfell House Museum** on the hillside above the centre, completed in 1910 and the actual Grenfell home. Behind the museum, there's a pleasant woodland path leading to the top of **Tea House**

St Anthony

Hill, where Grenfell and his wife were buried.

You should also make time for the remarkable ceramic **Jordi Bonet Murals** depicting the culture and the history of Newfoundland and Labrador inside the nearby Rotunda (the main entrance of the Charles S. Curtis Memorial Hospital), created by Montréal artist Jordi Bonet in 1967.

Dark Tickle Company

Allow time for the easy 40km drive north to L'Anse aux Meadows (around 35min non-stop via Rte-430 and Rte-436). On route you'll pass the fabulous **Dark Tickle Company** ❺ (www.darktickle.com) shop in tiny Saint Lunaire-Griquet, most famous for its local wild berry jams and preserves but also selling a wide-range of Newfoundland sauces, vinegars, teas, drinks, chocolates and arts and crafts.

You can also grab a light meal here, at the on-site **Café Nymphe** (see ❸; summer daily 9am–9pm). In L'Anse aux Meadows try and snag a room at **Jenny's Runestone House** (see page 108).

L'ANSE AUX MEADOWS NATIONAL HISTORIC SITE

In 1960 on the far northern tip of Newfoundland, a local named George Decker took Helge Ingstad, a Norwegian writer and explorer, to a group of grassed-over bumps and ridges beside Epaves Bay; the place was **L'Anse aux Meadows** ❻ (www.pc.gc.ca/en/lhn-nhs/nl/meadows; daily June–Sept 9am–5pm; $11.90), now a UNESCO World Heritage Designation, and the bumps turned out to contain the remnants of the only Norse village ever to have been discovered in North America.

Ingstad dug up the foundations of eight turf and timber buildings and a ragbag of archeological finds, including a bronze cloak pin (which provided the crucial carbon dating for the site), a stone anvil, nails, pieces of bog iron, an oil lamp and a small spindle whorl.

The Norwegian concluded that the remains were left behind by a group of about a hundred Viking sailors, carpenters and blacksmiths who probably remained at the site for just one or maybe two years, using it as a base for further explorations.

Begin day three at the **L'Anse aux Meadows visitor centre**, where the Norse artefacts appear alongside exhibitions on the background to the site as well as Viking life and culture. From here it's a few minutes' walk to the cluster of gentle mounds that make up what's left of the original village, and another short stroll to a group of full-scale replicas centred around a longhouse – costumed role-playing interpreters enhance the experience with demonstrations of traditional activities such as cooking, weaving and boat building.

Norstead Viking Village

Norstead

Just 2km from the original Viking settlement at L'Anse aux Meadows, **Norstead** ❼ (http://norstead.com; early June to mid-Sept daily 9.30am–5.30pm; $10) is an impressive replica of a Norse port replete with full-scale Viking ships, offering a touristy but extremely entertaining glimpse into Viking life a thousand years ago.

Costumed interpreters lead hands-on activities, tell stories in the chieftain's hall and demonstrate ancient crafts like spinning and pot making.

Before you leave the area, make sure you book a table at **The Norseman** (see ❹). This establishment makes for an exceptional dining experience, whether you choose to visit for lunch or dinner, with high-quality dishes on offer.

Food and Drink

❶ ANCHOR CAFÉ

10 Fisher St, Port au Choix; tel: 709-861 3665; daily 11am–9pm; $$
Friendly local diner overlooking Port au Choix harbour, built to look like a fishing boat and decorated with all sorts of nautical memorabilia inside. The seafood is always fresh – the moose burgers, traditional chowder (fish and shrimp), and the halibut or cod fish and chips are especially good, with bakeapple cheesecake usually on offer for dessert.

❷ LIGHTKEEPERS CAFÉ

21 Fishing Point Rd, St Anthony; www.facebook.com/Lightkeeperscafe; tel: 709-454 4900. Late May to early Oct daily 11.30am–9pm; $$
Located in the former home of the Fishing Point lighthouse keeper, dine on tasty Newfoundland seafood – lobster, crab, mussels, cod and the best crab cakes in the region – while enjoying the views of ocean, whales and icebergs.

❸ CAFÉ NYMPHE

75 Main St, St Lunaire-Griquet; www.darktickle.com; tel: 709-623 2354; daily 9am–9pm; $
Nautical-themed bistro attached to the Dark Tickle Company store and factory, serving homemade soup, sandwiches and daily specials, with desserts featuring locally grown wild berries (think "chocolate screech" cheesecake and blueberry crumble).

❹ THE NORSEMAN

Harbourfront, L'Anse aux Meadows; www.valhalla-lodge.com/restaurant; tel: 709-689 2126; late May to early Sept daily noon–8pm; $$
High quality restaurant overlooking the ocean, serving fish chowders, scallops in white wine sauce, baked cod with Dijon mustard sauce, local lamb, local berry pies and ultra fresh lobster, plucked from their own on-site supply. Drinks served with genuine iceberg ice.

The Trans–Labrador Highway

TRANS-LABRADOR HIGHWAY

One of the world's great highway adventures, the Trans–Labrador cuts through a vast untouched wilderness, from the historic villages along the Gulf of St Lawrence, across the Mealy Mountains to Happy Valley–Goose Bay and the heavily wooded interior of sub–Arctic Canada.

DISTANCE: 620km
TIME: 3 days
START: Blanc-Sablon, Québec
END: Happy Valley-Goose Bay, Newfoundland and Labrador
POINTS TO NOTE: This tour is designed as a road-trip, with most of the route paved by the end of 2022 – only 150km remains unpaved, with 80–100km contracted for paving in 2021. If you're renting, check your rental policy in advance, though firms no longer try to bar drivers from the roughest sections of the highway. Try Eagle River Rent-a-Car in Forteau (tel: 709-931 3300). The assumed start of this tour is Blanc-Sablon, just across the border in Québec, where the ferry from St Barbe in Newfoundland docks and the airport is located. Reservations are recommended for the ferry (1–3 daily; 1hr 45min; https://lmsi.woodwardgroup.ca) and all traffic must check in 1hr before departure. Reserve all accommodation (see page 108) in advance and always drive with your lights on.

One of the last great unspoiled adventure destinations, Labrador is home to the planet's largest herd of caribou, wandering polar bears, awe-inspiring waterfalls and a string of pristine coastal communities that have preserved a raw, 19th-century quality despite the onset of wi-fi and SUVs. The Trans-Labrador Highway also takes in a rich cultural heritage, passing two of the most important historic sights in Canada, Red Bay and Battle Harbour.

Labrador has been attached to Newfoundland politically since 1809, but it has a distinct identity, with a diverse ethnic mix of white settlers, Métis, Innu and Inuit; the Labrador flag is flown everywhere with pride (the self-governing Inuit region of Nunatsiavut in northern Labrador was created in 2005). Labrador constructed the Trans-Labrador Highway in stages from the 1970s to 2009, and it's now possible to drive across the entire province.

THE LABRADOR STRAITS

From the ferry dock or airport at tiny **Blanc-Sablon ❶** in Québec head east

Point Amour Lighthouse

into Labrador along the first section of the Trans-Labrador Highway (Rte-510), which connects a string of former fishing camps that are now modest villages huddling against the coastal cliffs in a region known as the Labrador Straits. The first community in Labrador itself is **L'Anse-au-Clair ❷**, settled by the French in the early 1700s, some 8km east of the Blanc-Sablon ferry terminal. Stop at the area's main source of information, the **Gateway to Labrador Visitor Centre** (mid-June to Sept daily 9am–6pm) housed in a former 1909 church. Another 10km northeast along Rte-510 is the village of **Forteau ❸**, at its liveliest during the annual three-day Bakeapple Festival in mid-August.

Point Amour

Continue 13km east (on Rte-510, then the signposted gravel L'Anse-Amour Rd) to the 36m-high **Point Amour Lighthouse ❹** (www.pointamourlighthouse.ca; early June to early Oct daily 9.30am–5pm; $6), which provides fabulous 360-degree views from the top of its 132-step tower. Completed in 1857 and still in use, its history and that of the whole straits region is laid out in the adjacent lightkeeper's quarters, staffed by costumed guides.

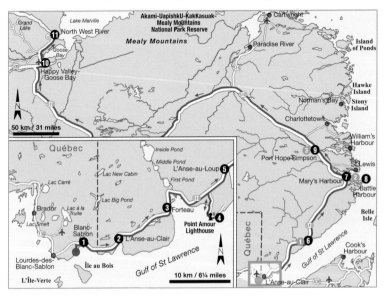

The Basque chalupa recovered from the waters of Red Bay, Interpretation Centre

L'Anse-au-Loup

A little further along Rte-510 in **L'Anse-au-Loup ⑤**, the **Labrador Straits Museum** (11 Branch Rd; www.labrador straitsmuseum.ca; early June to mid-Sept Mon–Sat 9.30am–5.30pm, Sun 1–5.30pm; $5) is an endearing collection of local relics and curios, mainly from the 1920s and 1930s. However, the story of the nearby 7500-year-old burial mound of a 12-year-old Archaic-Indian boy (the oldest-known funeral monument in North America), is also told in detail. You can see the mound itself – a well-defined heap of rocks – on the road from Point Amour Lighthouse.

Red Bay

It seems inconceivable today, but the sleepy village of **Red Bay ⑥** – 75km northeast of L'Anse-au-Claire on Rte-510 – was once the world's largest whaling port, occupied by Basque fishermen years before the arrival of the Pilgrims in New England. Despite the abundance of broken red tiles on the beaches, their presence here was eventually forgotten, and only rediscovered in the 1970s after obscure documents in Spain led to the astounding discovery of the remains of a Basque ship buried in the harbour. Grab lunch at **Whaler's Restaurant** (see ①) before exploring the **Red Bay National Historic Site** (www.pc.gc.ca/en/lhn-nhs/nl/redbay; early June to early Oct daily 9am–5pm; $11.90). Start at the reception centre,

Alternative Routes

To get an early start, stay the night at Northern Light Inn in L'Anse-au-Clair and begin this tour the following day. Though the tour ends at Happy Valley-Goose Bay, it's now relatively straightforward to continue to Churchill Falls and Labrador West at the end of Trans-Labrador, and even to carry on south into Quebec. As with Newfoundland, most sights in Labrador are only open fully in the summer months (June to September). A note about times zones: Happy Valley-Goose Bay is in the Atlantic Time Zone, but Southern Labrador is within the Newfoundland time zone, which is 30min later than Atlantic time. Blanc-Sablon in Québec also observes Atlantic Time, but does not observe Daylight Saving Time like the other two regions. This means that in summer, when its 6pm in Newfoundland and on the south coast of Labrador, it's 5.30pm in Happy Valley, but 4.30pm in Blanc-Sablon.

There is no cell/mobile phone service along the highway – instead you can borrow satellite phones for emergency use only (available at the Alexis Hotel in Port Hope Simpson, Riverlodge Hotel in Mary's Harbour, and Northern Light Inn in L'Anse au Clair). Residents of Newfoundland and Labrador must provide their driver's license, while others must provide a credit card number for replacement if the units are not returned.

Battle Harbour

where the discoveries are introduced with a 20-minute film and the most impressive relic is displayed: one of the small *chalupas* actually used by the whalers in the 1580s. Down the road, the interpretation centre contains two floors of artefacts recovered from the wrecks and nearby Saddle Island, which you can take a boat trip to (hourly departures from the interpretation centre daily 9am–4pm July–Sept; $3). Here you can roam around the eerie whalers' cemetery and other labelled sites on a self-guided tour.

MARY'S HARBOUR

Northeast of Red Bay, Rte-510 continues on for 85km up the coast to **Mary's Harbour ❼**. Founded in 1930 by a handful of families after a hospital fire at Battle Harbour began an exodus to the mainland, today it's a surprisingly vibrant little town, living primarily on the seasonal crab fishery and tourism. It's also a sensible place to spend the night, if you can afford it; the main attraction here is **Battle Harbour**, on tiny Battle Island some 9km offshore – signs lead through the village to the ferry dock. If you end up in Mary's Harbour, eat at **Connie's Bakery** (see ❷).

BATTLE HARBOUR

It's worth devoting a whole day to **Battle Harbour ❽** (https://battleharbour. com; usually open mid-June to mid-

Sept) either on a day-trip from Mary's Harbour or by spending one or two nights on the island. This beautifully restored fishing port is visited by towering icebergs in spring and humpback whales in summer; orca whales often cruise right off the dock. Established in the 1770s, Battle Harbour became one of the world's busiest saltfish, salmon and sealing ports in the 19th century, but a devastating fire in 1930 exacerbated long-term decline.

An epic restoration project by the Battle Harbour Historic Trust has resulted in a clutch of wonderfully evocative old wooden buildings opening to the public, a visitor centre and several walking trails; you can also stay in some of the old houses. Many of the former residents of the town serve as guides and are as equally absorbing as the site itself. Day trips to Battle Harbour are operated by Cloud 9 Boat Charters and Tours (15 Barney's Pond Rd; www. cloud9boattours.ca) in Mary's Harbour.

PORT HOPE SIMPSON

Get an early start on day three for the scenic 55km drive from Mary's Harbour to **Port Hope Simpson ❾**, another isolated community, founded in 1934 as a logging company town. This is your last chance for petrol and provisions before the long haul on Rte-510 to Happy Valley-Goose Bay. Eat at **Alexis by the Bay Restaurant** (see ❸). From here it gets serious – 405km of absolute wilder-

Overnight at Battle Harbour

Labrador Heritage Museum, North West River

ness (at least 7 hours non-stop) with no gas stations and no services of any kind (make sure you have one of the free satellite phones). The highway cuts through seemingly endless forest, south of the **Mealy Mountains**. Eventually the road crosses the mighty Churchill River and meets Rte-500 on the other side, from where it's a short drive east into **Happy Valley-Goose Bay** ❿.

HAPPY VALLEY-GOOSE BAY

Sandwiched between the Churchill River and the westernmost tip of sprawling Lake Melville, **Happy Valley-Goose Bay** is the principal transport and administrative hub of Labrador, as well as its largest settlement (with just over 8,000 people).

Happy Valley, where most of the shops and restaurants are located a few kilometres from the airfield, is a fairly quiet, laidback sort of place. Today you can visit the **Labrador Military Museum** on the old base (Canex building, 381 Banshee Blvd; July and Aug Mon, Tue, Thu and Fri 9am–noon and 1–4pm, Sat and Sun 1–4pm; free), which documents the history of the Canadian, British, American, Dutch and German military presence. For more history, visit the small Hudson Bay Company settlement of **North West River** ⓫, 38km to the north. For accommodation in Happy Valley see page 109.

Food and Drink

① WHALER'S STATION

72–76 West Harbour Drive, Red Bay; www.redbaywhalers.ca; tel: 709-920 2156; May–Sept Mon–Sat 10am–4pm, Sun 11am–5pm; $

The main restaurant in town, decorated with historic memorabilia, from old carvings and a Basque flag to ancient whalebones. It offers simple but hearty meals, like the classic "chalupa" fish and chips, plus homemade desserts made with local bakeapples, partridgeberries and blackberries.

② CONNIE'S BAKERY

35 Hillview Rd, Mary's Harbour; tel: 709-921

6959; Mon–Sat 9am–9pm; $

The only place to eat in Mary's Harbour is this small convenience store and bakery/sit-down restaurant run by Jason and Connie Simms. Bread is freshly baked daily, with sandwiches and light meals served.

③ ALEXIS BY THE BAY RESTAURANT

3 Alexis Drive, Port Hope Simpson; www.alexishotel.ca; tel: 709-960 0228; Jan 1–Dec 31 daily 8am–7pm; $$

Another hotel restaurant, with beautiful views across the Alexis River, with basic home-cooked meals from breakfast through dinner, from hot turkey sandwiches and burgers to basi pizza – they often run out of things, but do the best they can this far off the beaten path.

Actors at the Citadel

HALIFAX WALK

The capital of Nova Scotia and the largest city in the Maritimes, Halifax is jam-packed with lively pubs, historic buildings, seafood restaurants, a fabulous art gallery, museums dedicated to seafaring and immigration, and an entertaining boardwalk along the waterfront.

DISTANCE: 2.6km

TIME: 1 Day

START: Halifax Citadel National Historic Site

END: Canadian Museum of Immigration at Pier 21

POINTS TO NOTE: Many sights in Halifax are only open fully in the summer months (June to September); if you're planning to visit any of the museums or historic sites, avoid doing this walk Monday or Tuesday, even in summer, as sights may be closed on these days. The tour can easily be completed on foot; the walk up and down the Citadel hill is short but fairly steep, however, and it is possible to be dropped off at the top entrance by Uber or regular taxi (Casino Taxi tel: 902-429 6666). Ongoing COVID-19 restrictions may impact the opening times listed below – check websites to confirm if you plan to visit a specific sight. For accommodation in Halifax, see page 109.

Set beside one of the world's finest harbours, Halifax has become the financial, educational and transportation centre of the Maritimes, with its population of just under 400,000 making it almost four times the size of its nearest rival, New Brunswick's Saint John. Founded by British settlers led by first governor Edward Cornwallis in 1749, Halifax was primarily a fortified navy base well into the 19th century with most Haligonians, as the locals are known, at least partly employed in a service capacity. Today Halifax retains a compact, thriving centre, with artists, street performers and students from prestigious Dalhousie University adding a grungy, alternative balance to the bankers and fashionistas. This one-day jam-packed tour starts at Citadel hill and ends on the waterfront.

HALIFAX CITADEL NATIONAL HISTORIC SITE

Start this tour at the top of Citadel hill which dominates downtown, crowned by the **Halifax Citadel National Historic Site ❶** (5425 Sackville St; www.pc.gc.ca/en/lhn-nhs/ns/halifax; daily:

The Town Clock

May and mid-Sept to Oct 10am–4pm; June to mid-Sept 10am–4.30pm; $11.90, $7.90 in May, and mid-Sept to Oct). The present fortifications are Victorian; although it never saw action, the fort was garrisoned by the British until 1906, and by Canadian forces during the two world wars. Today it's an absorbing blend of museum, castle and historical re-enactment, with bagpipes blaring, marching "soldiers" of the Royal Artillery and 78th Highlanders in period kilts and uniform (c.1869), and an elaborate ceremony to fire one of the old cannons every day at noon, which makes a terrific bang. The fortification site is worth a visit for the grand view over the city and harbour alone. From here, walk back down into town via the Palladian **Town Clock** ❷ of 1803, a city landmark and obligatory photo op.

GRAND PARADE

From Brunswick Street at the foot of the Citadel walk down Carmichael Street to the **Grand Parade**, the city's genteel central square, bookended by the **City Hall** of 1890 and handsome **St Paul's Church** ❸ (1749 Argyle St; www.stpaulshalifax.org; Mon–Fri 9am–4.30pm; free). The chunky cupola and timber frame of the church date from 1750, making it both the oldest

City Hall

building in town and the oldest existing Anglican place of worship. The **cenotaph** in the centre of the Grand Parade was raised in 1929 to commemorate the Nova Scotians who died in World War I.

ART GALLERY OF NOVA SCOTIA

Walk down Prince Street from the church two blocks to Hollis Street – on your left (north) side is the must-see **Art Gallery of Nova Scotia ❹** (1723 Hollis St; https://artgalleryofnovascotia.ca; Mon–Wed and Fri –Sun 10am–5pm, Thu 10am–9pm; $12, free Thu 5–9pm), but if you want to have lunch first, just ahead of you on the right is the **Old Triangle Irish Alehouse** (see ❶), serving excellent pub grub and seafood. The Art Gallery occupies two adjacent buildings – one the stern Art Deco Provincial Building, the other an embellished Victorian edifice (the 1867 Dominion Building) that has previously served as a courthouse, police headquarters and post office. The gallery is attractively laid out and although there is some rotation of the exhibits most of the pieces described here should be on view.

Floor 1 of Gallery South (Provincial Building) contains a delightful section devoted to the Nova Scotian artist Maud Lewis (1903–70), portrayed by British actress Sally Hawkins in the 2016 movie *Maudie*. Lewis overcame several disabilities, including rheumatoid arthritis, to become a painter of some renown, creating naive, brightly coloured works of local scenes. Lewis's tiny "Painted House" – awash with her bright paintwork – was removed from the outskirts of Digby for safe-keeping in 1984, and was finally placed here in 1997.

An underground passageway connects the Lower Floor of Gallery South with the Lower Floor of Gallery North. Here you'll find Canadian historical paintings, while room 4 holds several canvases by Cornelius Krieghoff and a small sample of the work of the Group of Seven.

The elegant building across the street from the Art Gallery's main entrance is **Province House ❺**, where the Nova Scotian legislature has been meeting since 1819 – a cosy space that partly resembles a Georgian dining room rather than a provincial seat of government (for free tours visit https://nslegislature.ca)

HALIFAX HARBOURFRONT

If the weather is good devote the afternoon and early evening to strolling the pedestrian friendly Harbourwalk that runs along the lively waterfront of Halifax (just two blocks east along Prince Street from the Art Gallery). At just over 4km, it is one of the world's longest continuous boardwalks. It's lined with pubs, restaurants and shops and several kiosks offering ways to explore Halifax by bike, Segway, kayak or guided boat tours. The Harbourwalk is anchored

The harbourwalk

on one end by Casino Nova Scotia and on the southern end by the Canadian Museum of Immigration at Pier 21.

Maritime Museum of the Atlantic
In the middle of Harbourwalk is the absorbing **Maritime Museum of the Atlantic** ❻ (1675 Lower Water St; https://maritimemuseum.nova scotia.ca; May–Oct Mon and Wed–Sat 9.30am–5.30pm, Tue 9.30am–8pm; Nov–Apr Tue–Sat 9.30am–4pm, Sun 1–4pm; May–Oct $9.55, Nov–Apr $5.15). The ground floor holds a series of small displays, including one on the cataclysmic Halifax Explosion of 1917, illustrated by a first-rate video and another showing artefacts from Nova Scotia's numerous shipwrecks. Upstairs, a collection of small boats and cutaway scale models detail the changing technology of shipbuilding in the "Days of Sail", but it is the Unsinkable Ship that attracts most attention, a detailed display on the *Titanic*, which sank east of Halifax in 1912.

HMCS Sackville
Docked outside the museum are an early 20th-century steamship, the **CSS Acadia** (part of the museum) and the World War II corvette, **HMCS Sackville** ❼ (https://hmcssackville.ca; mid-June to late Oct daily 10am–5pm; $5). Canada's oldest fighting warship and the nation's official Naval Memorial, HMCS *Sackville* is the last of many convoy escort vessels built during World War II

– Halifax was a key assembly point for convoys during the Battle of the Atlantic. Exploring the cramped decks and interior, restored to their 1944 configuration, brings home just how grim the war at sea must have been. The **Halifax Waterfront Visitor Information Centre** ❽ (https://tourismns.ca/halifax-waterfront-visitor-information-centre; daily: June to Oct 9am–7pm; Nov–May 9am–4.30pm) stands on the Harbourwalk next to the ship.

Discovery Centre
From the Maritime Museum it's a 15-minute stroll along the Harbourwalk to the **Halifax Seaport** development (www.halifaxseaport.com) at the southern edge of downtown. On the way be sure to stop at **Beavertails** (see ❷), for a classic sweet treat, and **Rum Runners** ❾ (https://rumrunners.ca; May to mid-Oct daily 11am–5pm) to buy their classic, chocolate or whisky rum cakes. Families may want to stop by the **Discovery Centre** ❿ (1215 Lower Water; https://thediscoverycentre.ca; daily 10am–5pm; $15, children 3 and above $12), a hands-on science museum targeted primarily at children. Otherwise walk on to the nearby Farmers' Market (usually closes at 5pm weekdays) or the Canadian Museum of Immigration (till 5.30pm).

Halifax Seaport Farmers' Market
A short walk beyond the Discovery Centre lies the **Halifax Seaport Farmers'**

Canadian Museum of Immigration at Pier 21

Market ⓫ (Marginal Rd, Pavilion 22; www.halifaxfarmersmarket.com), a popular arts, crafts and artisan food market that moved into new digs in 2021; the market is open daily outdoors in the summer months, moving inside for winter (weekends only).

Canadian Museum of Immigration at Pier 21

Adjacent to the Farmers' Market is the Seaport's premier historic attraction, the **Canadian Museum of Immigration at Pier 21** ⓬ (1055 Marginal Rd; pier21.ca; Apr Tue–Sun 10am–5pm; May–Oct daily 9.30am–5.30pm; Nov daily 9.30am–5pm; Dec–Mar Wed–Sun 10am–5pm; $14.50). Around 1.5 million immigrants and Canadian military personnel passed through Pier 21 between 1928 and 1971, and the museum features recordings and video testimonies of many, enhanced with an assortment of interactive exhibits. Start with the 30-minute multimedia presentation (shown frequently), which features compelling dramatizations of immigrant arrivals from the 1920s to the 1960s. Just across from the museum is **Garrison Brewing** (see ❸), the perfect spot to end the day with a craft brew, or "seaport soda".

Food and Drink

❶ THE OLD TRIANGLE IRISH ALEHOUSE

5136 Prince St; www.oldtriangle.com; tel: 902-492 4900; Mon, Tue and Sun 11am–midnight, Wed and Thu 11am–12.30am, Fri and Sat 11am–2am; $$

An Irish-style pub with a whole network of cosy snugs and a warm and welcoming atmosphere. Serves a selection of Irish and Maritime dishes, from seafood chowder and pan-fried haddock, to lamb shank and Irish stew. Live music every night, with Celtic music most weekends.

❷ BEAVERTAILS

Harbourwalk, 1549 Lower Water St; https://beavertails.com; tel: 902-789 0989; May–Oct daily 11am–7pm; $

Deep-fried wholewheat dough, stretched to look like a beaver's tail, and smothered with sweet toppings; the original version is simply sprinkled with cinnamon and sugar, but the apple cinnamon, banana-chocolate and maple butter are totally addictive.

❸ GARRISON BREWING

1149 Marginal Rd; www.garrisonbrewing.com; tel: 902-453 5343. Sun–Thu noon–6pm, Fri noon–7pm, Sat 10am–7pm

Award-winning microbrewery near Pier 21 and the Farmers' Market, with tasty brews such as Imperial IPA, Jalapeño Ale and the raspberry wheat on tap. Opt for the sample tray if you can't decide.

Cabot Trail road seen from high above on the Skyline Trail

CAPE BRETON ISLAND: THE CABOT TRAIL

Cape Breton Island offers a tantalizing blend of exquisite mountain landscapes and a gorgeous coastline. Encircling most of the Cape Breton Highlands National Park is the Cabot Trail, reckoned to be one of the most awe-inspiring drives on the continent.

DISTANCE: 285km
TIME: 3 days
START: Buckwheat Corner (where Hwy-30 meets Hwy-105)
END: Baddeck
POINTS TO NOTE: As with the rest of Nova Scotia, most sights on Cape Breton are only open fully in the summer months (June to September). This tour is designed as a standalone road-trip – it can also be completed as loop from Baddeck. It's important to reserve all accommodation (see page 109) far in advance, as there's not a lot of choice; it's also best to reserve any whale-watching tours in advance. Note that Cape Breton's weather is notoriously unpredictable, even in summer. The Cabot Trail is pretty miserable in mist and rain, so if possible you should build a bit of flexibility into this itinerary.

The Cabot Trail begins at Hwy-105 (Exit 7) before weaving its way on a scenic loop around the northern tip of the island, passing through Cape Breton Highlands and ending in Baddeck, back on Hwy-105. Construction of the initial route was completed in 1932, named after the explorer John Cabot who landed somewhere in Atlantic Canada in 1497. Whale-watching cruises are big business hereabouts and they are available at almost every significant settlement from May to October when fin, pilot, humpback and minke whales congregate off the island. Cape Breton Island is also a major locus for Scottish culture; it attracted thousands of Scottish Highlanders at the end of the 18th century, and many of the region's settlements celebrate their Scots ancestry and Gaelic traditions in one way or another.

LA RÉGION ACADIENNE

The **Cabot Trail** (aka Hwy-30) begins to run north from Exit 7 on Hwy-105 (Trans-Canada Highway) at the tiny hamlet of **Buckwheat Corner** ❶. From here it's 54km through the Margaree Valley to **Margaree Harbour** ❷ on

the coast, where the Cabot Trail offers captivating views of land and sea as it slices north across the wide grassy littoral. The scattered dwellings hereabouts form **La Région Acadienne**, an Acadian enclave established in 1785 by French settlers deported from elsewhere in the Maritimes. Stop at the **Centre de la Mi-Carême ❸**, (www. micareme.ca; June–Aug daily 10am–5pm, Sept and Oct Wed–Sun 10am–5pm; $5) some 14km north of Margaree Harbour in Grand Étang, to learn about the French "Mi-Carême" carnival tradition. From here it's another 6km to **Flora's Gift Shop ❹** (http:// floras.com; June–Oct daily 9am–5pm), a huge emporium of local souvenirs and crafts, including the very popular hooked rugs.

Chéticamp
Just beyond Flora's, the road slips into the district's main village, **Chéticamp ❺**, its old centre dominated by the soaring silver steeple of l'**Église Saint-**

Pierre, completed in 1893 with stones lugged across the ice from Chéticamp Island, just offshore. Just along from the church, **L'abri** (see ❶), is a great,

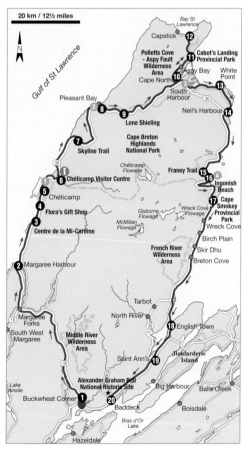

Autumn in Highlands National Park

no-frills spot for lunch, or you can first visit **Les Trois Pignons** a little further up the road (www.lestroispignons.com/en; daily: mid-May to June and Sept to mid-Oct 8.30am–5pm; July and Aug 8.30am–6.30pm; $5) which displays a collection of hooked rugs and Acadian crafts, and a full range of visitor information services. After lunch stop at the **Freya & Thor Gallery and Café** (mid-May to mid-Oct 9am–4pm) to admire the work of local artists (including the whimsical pieces of William Roach), and sip espresso.

CAPE BRETON HIGHLANDS NATIONAL PARK

From the gallery it's just 4km to the entrance of **Cape Breton Highlands National Park** (www.pc.gc.ca/en/pn-np/ns/cbreton; $7.90) – stop off at the **Chéticamp Visitor Centre ❻** (daily: late June to late Aug 8.30am–7pm; mid-May to late June and late Aug to mid-Oct 9am–5pm) to get the latest on park conditions and openings. The national park offers some of the most mesmerizing scenery anywhere in the Maritimes – a mix of deep wooded valleys, rocky coastal headlands, soft green hills and boggy upland. Although visitors get a taster of the park travelling by car, the essence of the place is only revealed on foot. The land bordering the Cabot Trail can be explored by 26 hiking trails signposted from the road, including wood-

land strolls and steeper climbs. One of the most popular is the **Skyline Trail ❼**, which clambers up the coastal mountains from a clearly marked trailhead on the road (at the top of French Mountain), 15km north from the visitor centre. The trail is 6.5km return, or 8.2km when completed as a loop – it follows a fairly easy, but allow two to three hours in total.

Pleasant Bay

Some 20km beyond the Skyline Trail lies the tiny village of **Pleasant Bay ❽** – if you skip the hike, you'll have time to visit the **Whale Interpretive Centre** (104 Harbour Rd; June to early Sept daily 10am–6pm; $5) here, and take one of the many whale-watching trips that run from the harbour (see Capt. Mark's Whale and Seal Cruise; www.whaleandsealcruise.com), though if you only have time for one whale-watching trip, wait until day two (see below).

Lone Shieling

Grab an early dinner in Pleasant Bay at the **Rusty Anchor** (see ❷), before making the final 29km run to **Cape North** (30min or so). On the way make a brief stop at the **Lone Shieling ❾**. The hut is on the northern perimeter of the national park in a valley that was settled by Scots in the early 1800s; it is accessible along a short and easy footpath from the road, providing a rare taster of the sugar maple hard-

wood forests that make up the park's central (and strictly protected) zone. For accommodation in **Cape North ⑩**, see page 109.

Gaelic Music

The Scottish Highlanders who settled much of the island in the late 18th and early 19th centuries brought with them strong cultural traditions. Today these are best recalled by the island's musicians, especially the fiddle players. Buddy MacMaster (1924–2014) was one of the greats, and current names to watch out for include his niece Natalie MacMaster, her cousin Ashley MacIsaac (special events only) and the remaining members of the Rankin Family, not to mention Glenn Graham, Rodney Mac-Donald and Jackie Dunn MacIsaac. Local tourist offices will gladly advise you on gigs, whether it be a ceilidh, concert or square dance, and listings are given in the weekly *Inverness Oran* (https://invernessoran.ca), a local newspaper available at tourist offices and convenience stores. During the summer there's something happening almost every day – the Saturday-night Family Square Dance at West Mabou Hall is especially well regarded (9pm–midnight; $10). The largest festival is Celtic Colours (https://celtic-colours.com), with performances all across Cape Breton held over 10 days in early to mid-October.

BAY ST LAWRENCE

Start day two by leaving the Cabot Trail to explore the **Cape North region**, the forested hunk of hill and valley that juts out into the sea where the Gulf of St Lawrence meets the Atlantic Ocean – aka "Top of the Island". Bay St Lawrence Road snakes north from the village of Cape North to tantalizing coves and isolated settlements. Try and reserve the first whale-watching trip at **Bay St Lawrence ⑫** itself, 17 miles from Cape North village; both **Captain Cox's Whale Watch** (www.whalewatching-novascotia.com; mid-June to early Oct, from 10.30am; $45) and **Oshan Whale Watch** (https://oshan.ca; Aug–Sept 10.30am and 4.30pm; $45) are highly recommended. Bay St. Lawrence is a rich feeding ground for long-finned pilot whales, white-sided dolphins, minke, humpback and fin whales, as well as grey seals, bald eagles, guillemots and cormorants. On the way it's worth stopping off at windswept **Cabot's Landing Provincial Park ⑪**, the spot where John Cabot may have "discovered" North America in 1497. Retrace your route back to Cape North and the Cabot Trail, then continue 4km east for lunch at **Danena's Bakery & Bistro** (see ③), right on the main road.

NEIL'S HARBOUR

It's worth taking another scenic detour off the Cabot Trail, 700m from *Dane-*

Ingonish Beach

na's, along **White Point Road**. This 18km coastal route takes in the picturesque fishing community of **White Point** ⑬ itself, and **Neil's Harbour** ⑭, where there's a lighthouse with an ice cream shop inside (cash only).

INGONISH

From Neil's Harbour, back on the Cabot Trail, it's around 28km to the community of **Ingonish Beach** ⑯, where a thin strip of silky sand faces South Bay, one of the most enticing beaches in the Maritimes. The easy 3.8km hike along **Middle Head** (drive through the grounds of Keltic Lodge to get there) offers sublime views across both South and North bays. Otherwise, tackle the **Franey Trail** ⑮, which cuts into Cape Breton Highlands National Park from a trailhead off the Cabot Trail in Ingonish Centre. It's a strenuous 7.4km loop, rewarded by panoramic views of the entire Clyburn Brook canyon and the Atlantic coast from Cape Smokey to Ingonish (2–3hr). Try and get a room at the **Keltic Lodge** (see page 109) – the on-site **Purple Thistle Dining Room** (see ④) is the best place for dinner.

THE GAELIC COAST

Day three begins with a drive south along the **Gaelic Coast** that takes in towering **Cape Smokey** just south of Ingonish Beach. **Cape Smokey Pro-** vincial Park ⑰, just off the road, features picnic tables, incredible views and a rough 5km (one-way) hiking trail. The Cabot Trail threads its way for around 60km down the coast from here to **St Ann's**, location of the **Gaelic College of Arts & Crafts** ⑲, but if the ferry is running it's more fun to take the shortcut along Hwy-312 via the **Englishtown Ferry** ⑱. The chief attraction at the Gaelic College campus is the **Great Hall of the Clans** (https://gaeliccollege.edu/visit/great-hall-of-the-clans; mid-June to Sept Mon–Fri 9am–4.30pm; $10), which provides Scottish Highland clan descriptions alongside exhibits, artefacts and models dressed in the appropriate tartan. Also inside are eight interactive displays highlighting other cultural aspects; you can even view *Faire Chaluim Mhic Leòid*, North America's first Gaelic-language short film.

BADDECK

Hwy-312 re-joins the Trans-Canada Highway (Hwy-105) just north of St Ann's, and it's then another 20km southwest to **Baddeck** ⑳. The laidback resort and yachting village enjoys a tranquil lakeside setting on St Patrick's Channel, an inlet of the tentacular **Bras d'Or Lake**. The village was founded by Irish and Scottish settlers in 1839, and today it has a year-round population of under a thousand. A very tranquil visit.

Lobster fishermen in Baddeck

Alexander Graham Bell National Historic Site

The primary attraction in Baddeck is the absorbing **Alexander Graham Bell National Historic Site** (559 Chebucto St; www.pc.gc.ca/en/lhn-nhs/ns/grahambell; late May to late Oct daily 9am–5pm; $7.90), which overlooks the water at the northern end of the village. The museum is a mine of biographical information about the Scottish-born Bell – who started spending his summers here in 1885 – and gives detailed explanations of all his inventions. Most famous for the invention of the telephone in 1876, Bell also worked on aircraft and boats, culminating in the first Canadian air flight here in 1909 – a replica of the Silver Dart is displayed in a special exhibit area. Bell's exploits culminated in 1919 with the launch of the world's first hydrofoil, the HD-4 (there's a full-scale replica as well as the original, in the same hall as the Silver Dart), which reached a speed of 114kmph on the lake in front of town. For accommodation in Baddeck, see page 109.

Food and Drink

① L'ABRI

15559 Cabot Trail Rd, Chéticamp; https://labri.cafe; tel: 902-224 3888; check hours online; $$$
High quality meals served in stylish digs overlooking the harbour, from Moroccan lamb to seafood sandwiches.

② THE RUSTY ANCHOR

23197 Cabot Trail Rd, Pleasant Bay; https://therustyanchorrestaurant.com; tel: 902-224 1313; July and Aug daily 11am–10pm, May, June, Sept and Oct daily 11am–8pm; $$
Log cabin style diner overlooking the ocean just outside Pleasant Bay, knocking out fresh chowder, clams, mussels, oysters and huge lobster rolls, as well as decent pastas, burgers and ribs, veggie options and homemade desserts.

③ DANENA'S BAKERY & BISTRO

30001 Cabot Trail Rd, Dingwall; tel: 902-383 2408; daily 11.30am–7.30pm; $$
Danena's daughters serve locally grown, seasonal produce as well as authentic Scottish baked goods and dishes (think turnip hash), burgers and poutine.

④ PURPLE THISTLE DINING ROOM

383 Keltic ln Rd, Ingonish Beach; www.keltic lodge.ca/dining/purple-thistle; tel: 902-285 2880; daily 8–10am and 6–9pm; $$$
Upscale dining experience in the Keltic Lodge, open for breakfast and dinner, enhanced by spectacular views of the Atlantic and surrounding hills. The evening menu includes items such as seared salmon, steak-on-a-bun and quinoa cakes.

Peggy's Cove

SOUTH SHORE AND THE ANNAPOLIS VALLEY

This three-day tour explores the southwestern half of Nova Scotia, blessed with dense forests, pretty fishing ports and small-town Atlantic Canada at its most romantic – rich in Acadian, British, French and Indigenous history.

DISTANCE: 295km
TIME: 3 days
START: Halifax
END: Annapolis Royal
POINTS TO NOTE: As with the rest of Nova Scotia, most sights on this road-trip are only open fully in the summer months (June to September). The best night to stay in Kejimkujik for activities is Saturday, but this trip can otherwise be completed any time of the week (in summer). It's also family-friendly, with plenty to interest the kids and relatively short drives between destinations. It's important to reserve all accommodation (see page 110) far in advance, especially at Kejimkujik National Park, and ideally all rentals and activities at "Keji" (as it is commonly known). Buy food and other supplies for your stay in Kejimkujik at Sobeys supermarket (421 Lahave St, Bridgewater; daily 7am–9pm), which is 18km west of Lunenburg, en route to the National Park.

The southern half of Nova Scotia has enough attractions to justify weeks of exploration, but this three-day itinerary provides an enticing taster, from the gorgeous fishing villages and coves of the Atlantic-wracked South Shore, across to the milder Annapolis Valley, crammed with reminders of its colonial past, as well incredible seafood and a burgeoning wine culture. In between lies the forests and pristine rivers of Kejimkujik National Park. Originally the home of the Mi'kmaq people, the French established the first permanent European settlement in these parts at Port Royal in 1605, laying the foundations for what would become French-speaking Acadia. The British established control over the region in the 18th century, and today the province displays mixed Acadian, English, Scottish and French heritage.

PEGGY'S COVE

From Halifax, Hwy-333 cuts south across thick woodland before reaching the South Shore, a winding ribbon of Atlantic fishing villages, glacial boulders and indented rocky bays beginning with tiny **Peggy's Cove ❶**, 45km from the capi-

tal. Founded in 1811, the hamlet, with a resident population of just 35 souls year-round, surrounds a rocky slit of a harbour, with the spiky Gothic Revival St John's Anglican Church of 1885, a smattering of clapboard houses and wooden jetties on stilts. As you enter the village, stop at the **Visitor Information Centre** (96 Peggy's Point Rd; http://peggyscoveregion.com; late May to late Oct daily 9am–5pm), which stocks local maps and heaps of information on the South Shore (and also has free wi-fi).

deGarthe Gallery

Opposite the information centre lies the **deGarthe Gallery** (109 Peggy's Point Rd; May–Oct 10am–4pm; $2). Finn-ish-born artist William deGarthe (1907–83) fell in love with Peggy's Cove in the 1930s, and moved here permanently in 1955. Today the gallery built next to his former home displays 65 of his paintings and sculptures. His dramatic **Fishermen's Monument**, carved into the 30m granite rock-face in the garden outside, is an epic tribute to local fishermen, unfinished at the time of his death.

Peggy's Point Lighthouse

It's a short walk or drive to the end of the road from here, where the solitary red-and-white striped **Peggy's Point Lighthouse** stands against the sea-smoothed granite of the shore – you can walk around the lighthouse but the inside is

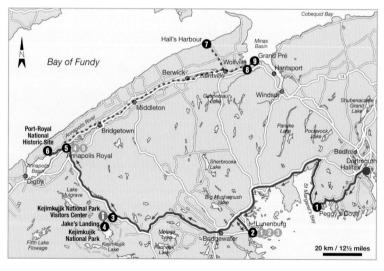

Luneburg

off-limits. Otherwise the main activity in Peggy's Cove is just wandering around the tiny harbour, soaking in the undeniable beauty of the place – try to get there early, before the coach tours arrive.

LUNENBURG

From Peggy's Cove it's around 100 winding kilometres to **Lunenburg ❷**, via Hwy-303, Hwy-103 and finally Hwy-324. Perched on a narrow, bumpy peninsula, Lunenburg is one of Nova Scotia's most beautiful towns, its central gridiron of streets clambering up from the main harbourfront flanked by elegant churches and candy-coloured wooden houses. Dating from the late 19th century, the most flamboyant of these mansions display an arresting variety of architectural features from Gothic towers and classical pillars to elegant verandas and the so-called "Lunenburg Bump", where triple-bell cast roofs surmount overhanging window dormers, giving the town a vaguely European appearance – which is appropriate considering it was founded in 1753 by German and Swiss settlers, dubbed the "Foreign Protestants", on invitation of the British in Halifax. Starting out as farmers, they eventually created a prosperous community of fishermen with its own fleet of trawlers and scallop-draggers – today the economy is still largely dependent upon the fishing industry, with lobster, scallop, haddock and halibut among the most popular fished, but

since being declared a UNESCO World Heritage Site in 1995 the tourism has boomed. Try and park on the waterfront, and grab lunch at **Salt Shaker Deli** (see ❶), before exploring the town.

Fisheries Museum of the Atlantic

Start at the **Fisheries Museum of the Atlantic** (68 Bluenose Drive; https://fisheriesmuseum.novascotia.ca; mid-May to June and Sept to mid-Oct daily 9.30am–5pm; July and Aug daily 9.30am–5.30pm; $14), housed in an old fish-processing plant by the quayside. The museum has an excellent aquarium, a room devoted to whales and whaling and displays on fishing and boat-building techniques.

Moored by the jetty, the real highlight is the *Theresa E. Connor*, a saltbank fishing schooner launched in 1938. Superbly restored, the schooner was one of the last boats of its type to be built, a two-masted vessel constructed to a design that had changed little since the early 18th century.

Knaut-Rhuland House Museum

Leave the waterfront on foot via King Street, turn right (east) on Pelham and visit the **Knaut-Rhuland House Museum** (125 Pelham St; www.lunenburgheritage society.ca/krhouse.htm; early June to Aug Mon–Sat 11am–5pm, Sun noon–4pm; Sept daily noon–4pm; free). This Georgian-style house was built around 1793 for wealthy merchant Benjamin Knaut, and is now staffed by guides dressed in

Luneburg's waterfront

period clothing. Free tours shed light on the items on display (working spinning wheels, some rare old German Bibles and antique furnishings). Take time also to view the exhibition room upstairs, which chronicles the history of the house and the town (Conrad Rhuland became the second owner in 1813), including the notorious Sack of Lunenburg in 1782 by US privateers from Boston. End the day with dinner at **Lincoln Street Food** (see ❷), and a night at one of Lunenburg's atmospheric inns (see page 110).

Historic Lunenburg

After breakfast at your hotel enjoy a morning stroll around Lunenburg, beginning at **St John's Anglican Church** (64 Townshend St; www.stjohnslunenburg. org; May and early Sept to early Oct Sat and Sun noon–4pm; June to early Sept daily 10am–7pm; donation $2), Lunenburg's most elegant building. Its original oak frame was imported from Boston in 1754, virtually destroyed by fire in 2001 and faithfully rebuilt in 2005 – it's a superb illustration of decorative Gothic. Walk down Cornwallis Street and turn left (east) at Pelham. Along this block (no.75) stands **Kaulbach House**, an inn that has changed little since its construction for one of the town's premier families in the 1880s. At heart, the house is a simple clapboard frame, but perky dormer windows have been tacked on, as has the triple-bell cast roof of the "bump". Continue walking east along Pelham to King Street, where you'll see the finest

of Lunenburg's mansions, the Zwicker House – now the **Mariner King Inn** – at no. 15. The house was built in 1830, but its exterior, including a fine example of the Lunenburg bump, was added later, probably in the 1870s.

Ironworks Distillery

Stroll on down to Montague Street and turn left (east), passing **Nº 9 Coffee Bar** (see ❸) and keep walking a few blocks east to the **Ironworks Distillery** (2 Kempt St; https://ironworksdistillery. com; Jan–Apr Thu–Sun noon–5pm; May to late June daily noon–5pm; late June to Aug daily 11am–7pm; Sept–Dec daily 11am–5pm). You can buy bottles of locally produced spirits here, as well as Pear Eau De Vie (brandy with a whole pear in the bottle), Annapolis apple vodka, and a rich apple brandy, aged in Hungarian oak barrels. Tours of the distillery are $15.

KEJIMKUJIK NATIONAL PARK AND NATIONAL HISTORIC SITE

From Lunenburg it's around 92km (1hr 15min) drive to **Kejimkujik National Park** ❸ (www.pc.gc.ca/en/pn-np/ns/ kejimkujik; park entry $5.90), in the densely wooded heart of the province. This magnificent tract of rolling wilderness, especially spectacular during the autumn foliage season, has a rich variety of forest habitat, interrupted by rivers and brooks linking about a dozen lakes; the main activities here are kayaking, biking and canoeing. In the spring the park is

Kejimkujik National Park

alive with wildflowers, whose brilliant colours provide cover for an abundance of porcupine, black bear, white-tailed deer and beaver, as well as three types of turtle. The Indigenous Mi'kmaq lived all over the Maritimes and in this region for centuries (discoveries along the Mersey River indicate that people used these local waterways 6,000 years ago). Despite the onset of European colonization, Kejimkujik remained important to the Mi'kmaq, and in 1842 12 plots of farmland were formally granted to Mi'kmaq families living on the shores of Kejimkujik Lake. Over 500 prehistoric Mi'kmaq petroglyphs can be seen in the park today, at several lakeshore locations.

Visitors Centre and Jake's Landing

Start at the **Visitors Centre** (late June to Aug daily 8.30am–8pm; late May to late June and Sept–Oct Mon–Thu 8.30am–4.30pm, Fri 8.30am–7pm, Sat and Sun 8.30am–6pm), which has detailed maps, an introductory film, exhibits and two short trails. Spend the rest of the afternoon exploring the park, on foot or by canoe. A couple of clearly defined canoe trips begin at **Jake's Landing** ❹ (8km south of the visitor centre). Canoes, kayaks and bikes can be rented from **Whynot Adventure** at Jake's Landing (mid-May to mid-Oct; www.whynotadventure.ca). While here, you should also try and take part in one of the **"Connect with Mi'kmaq culture"** programmes from the Acadia people for an illuminating glimpse into rich cultural traditions and myth – Mi'kmaq craftsman Todd Labrador builds traditional birch bark canoes on-site for example, and gives public demonstrations.

Spend the night in the park (see page 110) and enjoy a spectacular star-filled sky. The park-run **Merrymakedge Eatery** is open six days a week in July and August (usually 11am–6pm), and there's a small tuck shop in the park, but otherwise it's best to bring food and eat picnic-style. If you'd prefer a hotel bed, carry on to Annapolis Royal (about 40 minutes drive).

ANNAPOLIS ROYAL

Start day three with the 50km drive from Kejimkujik to **Annapolis Royal** ❺ via Hwy-8. With a population of just 600, this historic town spreads across a podgy promontory that lies tucked in between the Annapolis River and its tributary, the Allain River. The British – who had renamed the town again in honour of Queen Anne – expelled the Acadians in 1755, and the elegant wooden mansions you see today were built by Loyalist settlers in later years. Though its history may seem a little confusing, the current town is undeniably appealing, blessed with quality B&Bs, restaurants and antique shops.

Fort Anne National Historic Site

Edging St George Street just before it swings along the waterfront are the substantial remains of **Fort Anne National**

View of Annapolis Basin from Fort Anne

Historic Site (323 St George St; www. pc.gc.ca/en/lhn-nhs/ns/fortanne; late May to mid-Oct daily 9am–5.30pm; $3.90), whose grass-covered ramparts date from 1702. A few military buildings remain inside, but the most significant survivor is the old officers' quarters in the centre. The British built these in 1797 and, surmounted by three outsized chimney stacks, they now house a small museum. Inside there's a copy of the original charter by which James I incorporated "Nova Scotia" in 1621, and a cheerful community tapestry tracing the town's history.

Annapolis Heritage Society properties

The Annapolis Heritage Society (https:// annapolisheritagesociety.com) runs two historic properties on the waterfront opposite Fort Anne, a taster of old town life. The **O'Dell House Museum** (late May to early Oct, check website for current hours; $3) at 136 St George Street was built in 1869 as a tavern and now houses Victorian period rooms and the society's genealogy centre. Nearby, the **Sinclair Inn Museum** (late May to early Oct, check website for current hours; $3) further down the street at no. 230 was built around 1710, making it ancient by Canadian standards – displays inside highlight early building techniques and 10 "ghosts" of the people who once lived here (actually computer images of actors in period garb). **Fort Anne Café** (see ④), is a solid option for lunch, while

the best coffee in town is served by **Sissiboo Coffee Roaster** (see ⑤).

Annapolis Royal Historic Gardens

Hop back in the car after lunch for the short drive to **Annapolis Royal Historic Gardens** (441 St George St; https:// historicgardens.wordpress.com; daily 9am–5pm; $16, Nov–May by donation, closed Sun), which feature a string of enjoyable theme gardens, from formal Victorian gardens to an extensive rose collection in which the different varieties are arranged broadly in chronological order. There's also La Maison Acadienne, an authentic replica of an Acadian dwelling circa 1671. The whole site slopes gently down towards the Allain River, with a dyke-walk offering views of mudflats and salt marshes and also twisting through elephant grass, a reed imported by the Acadians to thatch their cottages.

PORT-ROYAL NATIONAL HISTORIC SITE

End your journey at the spot where it all started. In 1605, Samuel de Champlain and Pierre Sieur de Monts set up camp close to the current **Port-Royal National Historic Site** ⑥ (12.5km from the Historic Gardens in Granville Ferry; www.pc.gc.ca/en/lhn-nhs/ ns/portroyal; late May to mid-Oct daily 9am–5.30pm; $3.90), on the north side of the Annapolis River – Nova Scotia's first European settlement. This was a commercial venture; the *hab-*

Fort Anne Officers building   *Annapolis Royal*

itation was where the French would trade with the Mi'kmaq for furs. Champlain left in 1607 (going on to found Québec), and the outpost was looted and destroyed by a party of desperate English colonists from Virginia in 1613. The stronghold dominated the estuary from a low bluff, as does today's evocative replica, a painstaking reconstruction completed in 1940, relying solely on the building techniques of the early 17th century. Rooms inside have been furnished as they might have appeared at the time, with the Trading Room containing a selection of real beaver, bear, fox and raccoon hides. From Port Royal it's around 200km back to Halifax (2hr 15min), or you could take an extra day to visit **Hall's Harbour** ❼ (www.hallsharbour.org), **Wolfville** ❽ (www.wolfville.ca) and **Grand Pré** ❾ (www.pc.gc.ca/en/lhn-nhs/ns/grandpre).

Food and Drink

❶ SALT SHAKER DELI
124 Montague St, Lunenburg; www.saltshakerdeli.com; tel: 902-640 3434; Sun–Thu 11am–8pm, Fri and Sat 11am–9pm; $$
A great little diner in an 1863 clapboard with excellent views across the harbour, serving Propeller draught beers (brewed in Halifax), salads, Indian Point mussels, smoked seafood chowder and pizza.

❷ LINCOLN STREET FOOD
200 Lincoln St, Lunenburg; https://lincolnstreetfood.ca; tel: 902-640 3002; check website for current hours; $$$
Contemporary, modern diner helmed by chef Paolo Colbertaldo, featuring seasonal menus and locally-sourced ingredients: spiced beet cake with pecan cream, lamb and sweet potato pie, celeriac ravioli and more.

❸ Nº 9 COFFEE BAR
135 Montague St, Lunenburg; www.facebook.com/no9coffeebar; tel: 902-634 3204; daily 8am–3pm; $
Lunenburg's hip coffee shop sells fabulous espresso drinks (Java blend beans), teas, and delicious baked goods. Relax in the backyard garden.

❹ FORT ANNE CAFÉ
298 St George St, Annapolis Royal; https://fortannecafe.ca; tel: 902-532 5254; Mon–Sat 11am–6pm; $$
Friendly diner on the main drag in Annapolis, serving fresh seafood, burger, salads, steaks and local berry pies.

❺ SISSIBOO COFFEE ROASTER
262 St George St, Annapolis Royal; https://sissiboocoffee.com/cafe; tel: 902-640 3434; Mon–Sat 7.30am–4pm, Sun 9am–4pm; $
This local coffee roaster offers great views across the water and superb espresso drinks, plus local Ingles Farm Cider, and baked goods from Oak Haven Bakery and Guy & Marie's French Bakery.

View over the town

CHARLOTTETOWN WALK

The tree-lined streets of Charlottetown, the charming capital of Prince Edward Island, make for an eminently walkable day of sight-seeing, taking in architectural landmarks such as Province House and Beaconsfield House, the waterfront, seafood restaurants and tributes to Anne of Green Gables.

DISTANCE: 2km
TIME: 1 Day
START: Province House National Historic Site
END: Government House
POINTS TO NOTE: As with the rest of PEI, most sights Charlottetown are only open fully in the summer months (June to September). The tour can be completed on foot, though it's easy to call a taxi (City Taxi tel: 902-892 6567; Co-op Taxi tel: 902-892 1111). Uber is not yet available in PEI, but Kari is a local ride-share outfit (www.meetkari.com). Reserve Charlottetown Festival tickets in advance.

Pocket-sized Charlottetown has been the administrative and business capital of PEI since the 1760s. The French had established a small settlement here in 1720, but the British took control in 1758, during the French and Indian War – the French Acadian settlers were expelled. Charlottetown was officially founded in 1764, named after Queen Charlotte, the wife of King George II, with the current street grid laid out in subsequent years. During the American Revolution, Massachusetts privateers sacked the town (1775), but the city grew steadily thereafter, with the Charlottetown Conference of 1864 eventually leading to Canadian Confederation. Today it remains the most urbane spot on the island, its comfortable streets hemmed in by leafy avenues of clapboard villas and Victorian red-brick buildings. In small-island terms, it also offers a reasonable nightlife, with a handful of excellent restaurants and a clutch of lively bars, though the best time to be here is in the summer, when the otherwise sleepy town centre is transformed by festivals, live music and street cafés. This walking tour takes in the best of the city sights.

Province House National Historic Site

Start your tour at Prince Edward Island's most significant historical attraction, the **Province House National Historic Site** ❶ (165 Richmond St; www.pc.gc.ca/en/lhn-nhs/pe/provincehouse; check website for latest opening times). Com-

Clapboard building　　　　　　　　　　　　　　　　　*Victoria Row*

pleted in 1847, the elegant neoclassical pile has been the seat of Prince Edward Island's provincial legislature ever since, but is best known for being the birthplace of Confederation. It was here that the Fathers of Confederation – representatives of Nova Scotia, New Brunswick, then-Canada (Ontario and Québec) and PEI – met during the Charlottetown Conference in 1864, to discuss a union of the British colonies in North America. It took two more conferences before the Dominion of Canada was finally proclaimed in 1867, though PEI didn't join for a further six years. Today Prince Edward Island's unicameral Provincial (Legislative) Assembly still meets here. Dennis King's Progressive Conservative Party has been in charge since 2019, with the Green Party forming the primary opposition (the first time a Green Party has earned that position in Canadian history). A major restoration project has been ongoing at Province House since 2018 – it should be complete sometime in 2022, but until then, visit the adjacent Confederation Centre of the Arts (see below) for exhibits on the site.

Confederation Centre of the Arts
Built in a Brutalist style 1964, the **Confederation Centre of the Arts ②** (145

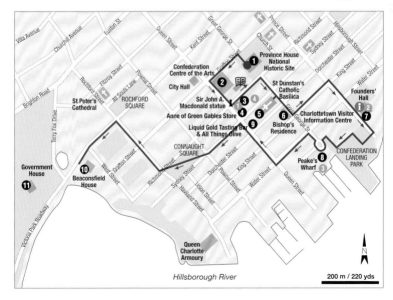

Colorful houses on Great George St

Richmond St; https://confederation-centre.com) is the home of the annual Charlottetown Festival and Anne of Green Gables musical, the island's main library, a couple of theatres, and an eclectic art gallery (mid-May to mid-Oct daily 9am–5pm; mid-Oct to mid-May Wed–Sat 11am–5pm, Sun 1–5pm; donation suggested), whose changing exhibitions always have a Canadian emphasis and often include a variety of 19th-century artefacts.

It's also the temporary home of the **Story of Confederation** exhibit (July and Aug Mon–Sat 9am–5pm, Sun noon–5pm; June, Sept and Oct Mon–Sat 10am–3pm; Nov–May Sat 10am–3pm; free), until at least 2022, which contains a replica of the Confederation Chamber where the Fathers of Confederation met in 1864, and shows the 20-minute film Building of Destiny.

Anne Of Green Gables: The Musical
Anne Of Green Gables: The Musical is Canada's longest-running show (although cancelled in 2020 and likely for 2021 due to the ongoing Covid pandemic), first performed at the Confederation Centre of the Arts in 1965. Based on the 1908 novel Anne of Green Gables by Lucy Maud Montgomery, the musical was originally created for TV in 1956. Today it remains a phenomenally popular event, with young actors from all over Canada vying for the lead role – Toronto-based performer Emma Rudy became the 19th Anne Shirley in 2019.

VICTORIA ROW

On leaving the Confederation Centre make for the corner of Queen and Richmond streets, the beginning of **Victoria Row ③**. This stretch of Richmond Street contains the finest examples of commercial architecture in the city, a long and impressive section that now holds a series of restaurants and bars; in the summer the whole street is pedestrianized and smothered with alfresco diners. Before wandering along the street, check out the bronze statue of the nation's first Prime Minister, **Sir John A. Macdonald**, placed here in 2009, casually sitting on a bench (it's an iconic photo spot). Also here, the **Anne of Green Gables Store ④** (110 Queen St; https://anne store.ca) is crammed with souvenirs and memorabilia of PEI's favourite literary heroine (**Anne of Green Gables Chocolates** is just down Queen Street at no. 100; https://annechocolates.com). On Victoria Row itself, **Receiver Coffee** (see ❶), is a good place for a pitstop.

ST DUNSTAN'S CATHOLIC BASILICA

At the end of Victoria Row turn right on Great George Street and walk by its the pretty terraced houses to **St Dunstan's Catholic Basilica ⑤** (45 Great George St; www.stdunstanspei.com; daily 8am–5pm). Finished in 1919 with twin spires and an imposing facade, the church has all the neo-Gothic trim-

St Dunstan's Basilica

Peakes Wharf

mings, from lancet windows to heavy-duty columns and a mighty vaulted ceiling. Just to the south of the church lies the stately **Bishop's Residence ⑥**, an Italianate and Gothic Revival influenced beauty completed in 1875. It's now owned by St. Dunstan's University (SDU). Turn left on King Street to admire some of Charlottetown's most historic clapboard and brick buildings before turning right on Prince Street and heading for the waterfront.

FOUNDERS' HALL AND PEAKE'S WHARF

Most of **Founders' Hall ⑦** on Charlottetown's harbourfront, has been transformed into a food hall and market (6 Prince St; https://foundersfoodhall.com; daily 9am–5pm, most vendors open Wed–Sat 11am–4pm, Sun noon–5pm) – grab lunch here (see ②). You'll also find **Charlottetown Visitor Information Centre** inside (www.discovercharlottetown.com; daily 9am–5pm). From Founders' Hall you can wander across to **Peake's Wharf ⑧**, a small collection of shops and restaurants on the waterfront. The development takes its name from "Peake No. 3 wharf", completed in 1872 by the Peake brothers, members of a successful PEI shipping family (the wharf originally extended further into the harbour). The four former outbuildings that remain today were built after 1904. Grab an ice cream at local favourite **Cows** (see ③).

BEACONSFIELD HOUSE

From Peake's Wharf it's a pleasant 1.2km stroll to beautiful Beaconsfield House, but it's also easy to call a taxi if legs are tiring. The walk takes you north along Queen Street, the city's main drag; at 72-74 Queen Street stop to admire an excellent example of pre-1860s Charlottetown commercial architecture, built for local shipping magnate James Duncan in 1855. Today half the building is occupied by **Liquid Gold Tasting Bar & All Things Olive ⑨** (www.allthingsolive.ca; Mon–Sat 10am–5pm), a little homage to the Mediterranean with samples of its fresh, extra virgin olive oil and balsamic vinegars from Modena, Italy. From here walk southwest along Sydney Street, and cut across landscaped Connaught Square to Rochford Street. Walk north up Rochford then left again at Kent Street. **Beaconsfield House ⑩** (2 Kent St; www.peimuseum.ca; May and June Mon–Fri 10am–4pm; July and Aug daily 10am–4.30pm; Sept and Oct Tue–Sat 10am–4.30pm; Nov–Apr Tue–Fri noon–4pm; $6) is a resplendent, late Victorian mansion, built in 1877 for James Peake, one of Charlottetown's leading shipbuilders (he went bust five years after its completion). The house changed owners and roles several times thereafter (it served as a "young ladies' residence" and later a dormitory for student nurses), until a local conservation society returned it to its former

Government House

glory in the 1970s. It occupies a magnificent site, overlooking the harbour.

GOVERNMENT HOUSE

A little further along Kent Street lies the manicured grounds and estate belonging to grandiose **Government House** ⓫ (1 Government Drive; www.lgpei.ca/history/government-house; July and Aug Mon–Fri 10am–3.30pm), a splendid neo-classical pile completed in 1834 and also known as Fanningbank (the land was originally set aside by Governor Edmund Fanning in 1789, the rest of his gift forming adjacent Victoria Park). It is still the Lieutenant-Governor's residence and only open for guided tours in July and August. The current Lieutenant Governor of Prince Edward Island is Antoinette Perry, appointed in 2017, an Acadian and former schoolteacher from Tignish. End the day with dinner and drinks at **Claddagh Oyster House** (see ❹) – if it's summertime (June–Aug), take in a **Charlottetown Festival** performance (https://confederationcentre.com).

Food and Drink

❶ RECEIVER COFFEE CO

128 Richmond St; www.receivercoffee.com; tel: 902-367 3436; daily 8am–3pm; $
Excellent coffee shop with an enticing patio and a range of quality espresso, as well as full breakfasts (*huevos rancheros* to banana rum French toast) and sandwiches for lunch.

❷ FOUNDERS' FOOD HALL

6 Prince St; https://foundersfoodhall.com; Wed–Sat 11am–4pm, Sun noon–5pm; $
Charlottetown's food hall offers a variety of tasty options, including Big Burger, Doughnuts by Design, Famous Peppers Fiamma (pizza), Receiver Coffee, Stir it Up (vegan), and Pour Authority (craft beer).

❸ COWS PEAKE'S WHARF

Peake's Wharf (Great George St);
https://cows.ca; tel: 902-566 4886; May–Oct daily 10am–5pm; $
Island institution, serving totally addictive ice cream in creative flavours like Wowie Cowie (vanilla, toffee, crunch and choc flakes) and Gooey Mooey. You can also tour the factory, on the North River Causeway (Rte-1).

❹ CLADDAGH OYSTER HOUSE

131 Sydney St (beneath the Olde Dublin Pub); https://claddaghoysterhouse.com; tel: 902-892 9661; Mon–Thu 5–9pm, Fri and Sat 5–10pm (open Sun 5–10pm May–Sept); $$
Attractive modern restaurant set in a red-brick Victorian, specializing in delicious PEI oysters. Otherwise, the menu offers a selection of seafood (fried crab and lobster cakes; salmon; butter-glazed halibut) and PEI beef dishes.

Red sands at Argyle Shore

PEI ROAD-TRIP

This three-day road-trip takes in the best of Prince Edward Island, with its charming villages and rolling farmlands, gorgeous beaches of red-hued sand, and the rich legacy of Anne of Green Gables – not to mention some of the finest seafood in Canada, from all-you-can-eat mussels, scallops, and chowder to fresh lobster suppers.

DISTANCE: 250km
TIME: 3 days
START: Charlottetown
END: West Point Lighthouse
POINTS TO NOTE: As with the rest of the Maritimes, most sights on Prince Edward Island are only open fully in the summer months (June to September). Unless you're planning a cycling holiday, you'll need a car to make the most of PEI – all the major rental agencies have offices at the airport or in Charlottetown. For accommodation, see page 110.

Prince Edward Island (PEI) is a real surprise, a land of rich, red earth, gently rolling farmland and neat villages of Victorian homes. Visit in the summer and it really does seems like a rustic oasis, little changed since local-born novelist Lucy Maud Montgomery described the island floating "on the waves of the blue gulf, a green seclusion and haunt of ancient peace". Even today, Canada's smallest province remains thoroughly agricultural, with Islanders remarkably successful in controlling the pace of change. Fish and lobsters are still sold off fishing boats, everyone seems to know everyone else and there are no freeways. The French settled what they called Île-St-Jean in the 1720s, but the British turned them out in the 1760s and renamed the island after the fourth son of King George III in 1799.

ARGYLE SHORE PROVINCIAL PARK

From Charlottetown, head 30km southwest via Rte-1 to **Argyle Shore Provincial Park ❶**, home of Prince Edward Island's quintessential "Red Sands Shore" – crumbling rust-red cliffs and red-sand beaches. If it's low tide visit nearby Canoe Cove (9km along Rte-19) at **Lloyd Inman Memorial Park ❷**, where tidal pools teem with marine life.

VICTORIA

From Argyle Shore it's just 11km along the Red Sands Shore route to the charming old seaport of **Victoria ❸**, overlooking the Northumberland Strait. Argyle

Shore is a good place for a picnic, but you can otherwise grab lobster rolls in Victoria at the **Lobster Barn Pub & Eatery** (see ❶). Don't miss **Island Chocolates** (7 Main St; www.islandchocolates.ca; July–Sept daily 9am–6pm), producer of Belgian-style handmade chocolates and fine coffee, as well as a wicked hot chocolate. Check out the **Victoria Seaport Lighthouse Museum** (2 Russell St; July to mid-Oct daily 10am–4pm; $1) or take a kayaking tour with **By-The-Sea-Kayaking** (www.bytheseakayaking.ca). In the evening catch a performance at the historic **Victoria Playhouse** (https://victoriaplayhouse.com; late June to late September). For accommodation in Victoria, see page 111.

PRINCE EDWARD ISLAND NATIONAL PARK

Start day two with the 40km drive northeast to **Brackley Beach ❹** in **Prince Edward Island National Park** – swim or just lounge on the powdery white sands and dunes. The gorgeous sandy beaches of the park actually extend along the Gulf of St Lawrence shore for some 40km. The Brackley Beach section lies at the northern terminus of Rte-15, but you can also turn left (west) along the coast

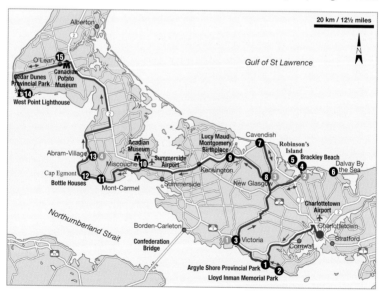

Beautiful rolling countryside arond Cavendish

for the causeway over to wooded **Robinson's Island ⑤** (home to the Robinsons Island Trail System, designed for mountain-bikers and hikers), or right (east) for the 5km trip along the seashore to Stanhope Beach and historic **Dalvay By the Sea ⑥**.

Dunes Studio Gallery and Café

After the beach, head south again on Rte-15, stopping at the nearby **Dunes Studio Gallery and Café** (see ②; 3622 Brackley Point Rd; http://dunesgallery.com; daily: May and Oct 9am–6pm; June and Sept 9am–8pm; July and Aug 9am–9pm), to peruse the pottery, art and lovely gardens. Grab lunch here if you skipped the picnic.

CAVENDISH

From Dunes Studio it's a pleasant 25km drive to **Cavendish ⑦**, home of Canada's favourite fictional heroine, **Anne of Green Gables**. As a result this is likely to be the most congested part of the island on your trip. Fans will love the attractions here, but even the uninitiated will appreciate the old houses (and the genuine enthusiasm of the local guides). The primary Anne pilgrimage site is **Green Gables Heritage Place** (8619 Cavendish Rd; www.pc.gc.ca/en/lhn-nhs/pe/greengables; May–Oct daily 9am–5pm; $7.90; May, June, Sept and Oct $6.40), the real farm owned by the Macneill cousins of Lucy Maud Montgomery that served as inspiration for the fictional Green Gables in the novels she started publishing in 1908. The rooms have been decked out in authentic period furnishings, though few pieces are original to the house – the main aim was to faithfully match descriptions in the book, and "Matthew's bedroom", the parlour and "Anne's room" are littered with items fans will recognize from the books. You can also explore the replica outhouses, and the visitor centre, which contains Montgomery's original typewriter and scrapbooks. Lucy died in Toronto, but was buried back on the island – the ceremony held here in 1942 is said to have been the closest thing to a state funeral PEI has ever had.

Confederation Trail

Prince Edward Island's quiet roads and gentle terrain make it a great place for cycling. In Charlottetown, Outer Limit Sports (330 University Ave; www.ols.ca/mystore; Mon–Fri 9am–5pm, Sat 9am–5pm) and MacQueen's (430 Queen St; www.macqueens.com; Mon–Sat 8.30am–5pm) rent out all the necessary gear, offer shuttles and will advise on trails. The most popular of these is the 273km Confederation Trail (http://tourismpei.com/pei-confederation-trail), a combined hiking and cycling trail that weaves its way across the heart of the island from east to west. You won't see much of the coast from the trail, but it's a wonderful way to take in the idyllic countryside.

The birthplace of Lucy Maud Montgomery

Avonlea Village

Families may want to check out **Avonlea Village** (8779 Cavendish Rd; http://avonlea.ca; daily: July and Aug 10am–8pm; Mid-June to end-June and Sept 3 to mid-Sept to 10am–5pm; free), a mock 19th-century village based on Anne of Green Gables' fictitious home. The site does contain three originals: the Belmont School, where Montgomery taught in 1896; Long River Church; and the old Clifton Manse from New London.

NEW GLASGOW

End the day at tiny **New Glasgow** ❽, 10km southeast from Cavendish on Rte-13. Check out the **Prince Edward Island Preserve Company** (2841 New Glasgow Rd; https://preservecompany.com; check the website for hours) for local jams, mustards and maple syrups. Aim to experience a PEI dining tradition here this evening at **New Glasgow Lobster Suppers** (see ❸), before spending the night at **FarmHouse Inn PEI** (see page 110).

LUCY MAUD MONTGOMERY BIRTHPLACE

Today the route runs "Up West" via the North Cape Coastal Drive, but Anne fans may want to stop off first at the **Lucy Maud Montgomery Birthplace** ❾ (http://lmmontgomerybirthplace.ca; mid-May to early Oct daily 9am–5pm; $5), in New London, 14.5km northwest from New Glasgow (Rte-224 then Rte-6). This lovely old clapboard house is where the author was born in 1874, and has been decked out with period furniture, personal scrapbooks and a replica of Montgomery's wedding dress.

LA RÉGION ÉVANGÉLINE

Keep driving west on Rte-6 then Rte-2 to pick up the North Cape Coastal Drive in **Miscouche** ❿, 30km from New London. This traditionally French part of the island was settled by Acadians in the 18th century and is known as **La Région Évangéline** (http://regionevangeline.com). Miscouche is home to the informative **Acadian Museum** (23 Main Drive; www.museeacadien.org; July and Aug daily 10am–5pm; Sept–June Mon–Fri 10am–5pm, Sun 1–4pm; $5.50). Continuing west on Rte-11, the **Cap Egmont headland** is a major centre of Acadian settlement, with tiny **Mont-Carmel** ⓫ dominated by the incongruous red-brick mass of the **Église Notre-Dame** (July and Aug daily 9.30am–6pm; free). Some 5km further along, the Acadian village of Cap-Egmont is home to the island's quirkiest sight, the **Bottle Houses** ⓬ (https://bottlehouses.com; mid-May to mid-Oct 9am–8pm; $8), built from around 30,000 bottles. Rte-11 continues on around the headland for 11km to **Abram-Village** ⓭, where the **Village Musical Acadien** cultural centre runs **La Trappe** (see ❹) restaurant.

View from the Lighthouse at West Point

WEST POINT

From Abram-Village the drive along the North Cape Coastal Drive to the **West Point Lighthouse** ⓭ on the far western tip of the island is 63km (1hr non-stop), but if there's time detour to the enlightening **Canadian Potato Museum** ⓮ (www.canadianpotatomuseum.info; mid-May to mid-Sept daily 10am–5.30pm; $10) in **O'Leary** to learn about PEI's all important potato crop. Once at West Point itself, visit the remote and windswept **West Point Lighthouse Museum** (June–Sept daily 9am–8.30pm; $5). Built in 1875, the 20m-tall lighthouse primarily functions as an unusual hotel today and is a great place to end your tour (see page 111), but non-guests can also climb to the top. The beach below the lighthouse is part of **Cedar Dunes Provincial Park**, one of the most enticing on the island.

Food and Drink

① LOBSTER BARN PUB & EATERY
19 Main St, Victoria; www.facebook.com/lobsterbarnpubandeatery; tel: 902-658 2722; May–Sept Tue–Sun 11am–7.30pm; $
Waterside restaurant utilising local seafood and organic veggies, with its lobster roll the star attraction, but equally tasty clams, veggie burgers, lobster poutine and excellent salads.

② DUNES STUDIO GALLERY AND CAFÉ
3622 Brackley Point Rd (Rte-15), Brackley Beach; http://dunesgallery.com; tel: 902-672 1883; daily: June and Sept 11.30am–7pm; July and Aug 11.30am–10pm; Oct 1 to mid-Oct Sun–Thu 11.30am–4.30pm, Fri and Sat 11.30am–7pm; $$
This gallery and shop also serves as café offering mouthwatering snacks and meals from an imaginative menu (PEI lobster asparagus quiche, Balinese pork and pineapple *nasi goreng*) that also includes plenty of vegetarian dishes.

③ NEW GLASGOW LOBSTER SUPPERS
604 Rte-258, New Glasgow; https://peilobstersuppers.com; tel: 902-964 2870; late May to Sept daily 4–8pm; $$
These famed lobster suppers have been running since 1958, with the usual gut-busting line-up of home-made rolls, seafood chowder, mussels and salad before the main event and ending with the "mile-high" lemon meringue pie.

④ RESTO-BAR LA TRAPPE
1745 Rte-124, Abram-Village; www.villagemusical.ca; tel: 902-854 3300; mid-June to mid-Sept daily 11am–7pm; $
This Acadian cultural centre runs a family restaurant serving delicious Acadian favourites such as the potato-pie-like râpure, clam pie, fish cakes and fresh mussels. You can buy cakes and pastries at La Galette Blanche Bakery on-site (same hours).

A STROLL AROUND SAINT JOHN

This walking tour takes in the best of Canada's oldest incorporated city, from the excellent provincial museum, architectural gems and tempting food stalls at City Market, to the bizarre phenomenon of the Reversing Falls Rapids.

DISTANCE: 4.4km
TIME: 1 Day
START: Art Warehouse
END: Reversing Falls Restaurant
POINTS TO NOTE: As with the rest of the Maritimes, most sights in Saint John are only open fully in the summer months (June to September); if you're planning to visit any the museums or historic sites, avoid doing this walk Monday to Wednesday, even in summer, as sights are often closed on these days. The tour can be completed on foot, with a 3km stroll on the last leg to the Reversing Falls: if legs are tiring, take a taxi; city buses also run from King's Square along King Street to the rapids (see https://saintjohn.ca/en). Ongoing COVID-19 restrictions may impact the opening times listed below – check websites to confirm if you plan to visit a specific sight. For accommodation in Saint John, see page 106.

The largest city in New Brunswick, Saint John is better known for its industrial prowess than its tourist attractions, home to iconic products such as Moosehead beer, the mighty Irving group of companies and a booming oil and gas sector. Yet the surprisingly compact downtown area is crammed with diverting sights, from resplendent Victorian architecture to the absorbing New Brunswick Museum and the Reversing Falls Rapids on the St John River, a dramatic spot to see the effects of the Fundy tides.

The French established a trading post here in 1631, but the city proper was founded by Loyalist refugees from the American Revolutionary War (1775–83). Some 15,000 United Empire Loyalists ended up in New Brunswick. Many had been subjected to reprisals by their revolutionary neighbours and most arrived virtually penniless. They and their descendants formed the kernel of powerful commercial and political cliques in the city. As a result, the Loyalists have frequently – and not altogether unfairly – been pilloried as arch-conservatives. In fact they were far from docile royalists:

Saint John from the Reversing Falls Park

shortly after their arrival in Canada they were pressing the British for their own elective assemblies. In the 19th century Saint John thrived on the lumber and shipbuilding industries, and despite a devastating fire in 1877, it was sufficiently wealthy to withstand the costs of immediate reconstruction. Consequently, almost all the city's older buildings – at their finest in the Trinity Royal Historic Preservation Area – are late Victorian.

Most of the action in Saint John takes place in the downtown area, known here as Uptown – the part of the city across the harbour is dubbed West Side.

TRINITY ROYAL HISTORIC PRESERVATION AREA

Start the day right with breakfast or coffee in the **Art Warehouse** (see **1**), a hip cafe, gallery, and drop-in art studio on Prince William Street, in the heart of **Trinity Royal Historic Preservation Area 1**. After the fire of 1877, the city's merchant class funded an ambitious rebuilding programme, epitomized by the brimmingly self-confident structures that grace this part of the city. The Art Warehouse itself occupies the Italianate **Jarvis Building**, a red-brick beauty completed in 1878.

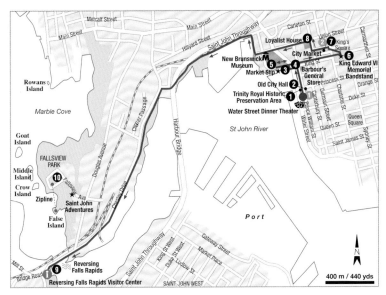

Heritage buildings

The grandiose building next door at 116 Prince William Street is the 1879 **Old City Hall** ❷, with a fine Second Empire sandstone façade, home of the city government up to 1971. On the other side of the street (no.115) is the similarly grand Second Empire **Old Post Office** of 1881, while the **Bank of New Brunswick Building** at no. 125 was completed in 1879 with a handsome Greek Revival facade of Corinthian columns. From here it's a short walk two blocks north along Prince William to Market Slip.

MARKET SLIP

The tiny rectangular dock at the foot of King Street, known as the **Market Slip** ❸, is where Saint John's founding 3,000 Loyalists disembarked in 1783. The Slip no longer functions as a port, but is still at the heart of Saint John, with warehouses converted into wine bars, restaurants and boutiques that front the modern Market Square shopping mall behind. Opposite is **Barbour's General Store** ❹ (10 Market Slip; late June to early Oct Thu–Sat 10am–6pm, Sun noon–6pm; free), an emporium that operated between 1860 and 1940 in Sheffield, New Brunswick, and is now stuffed with Victorian paraphernalia (you can also buy chocolates from New Brunswick's Ganong here).

It also operates as a **Visitor Information Centre**, and at the back the self-serve Exchange offers Java Moose Coffee, King Cole teas from Barbour's, and tasty oatcakes from the Cape Breton Oatcake Society. Incidentally, the small red and white lighthouse at the end of the Market Slip dock is actually a fake, built in 1985 by the adjacent Coast Guard base.

NEW BRUNSWICK MUSEUM

Head into the Market Square shopping mall to visit the enlightening **New Brunswick Museum** ❺ (www.nbm-mnb.ca; Mon–Wed and Fri 9am–5pm, Thu 9am–9pm, Sat 10am–5pm, Sun noon–5pm; Nov to mid-May closed Mon and Sun; $8). The museum contains an especially revealing section on the province's lumber, industrial and shipbuilding traditions as well as a fine collection of Chinese decorative and applied art. There's also much on the region's marine life, including the skeleton of a rare North Atlantic Right whale, and a 13m-high tidal tube constructed to illustrate the rise and fall of the Bay of Fundy tides.

KING'S SQUARE

Back outside on Market Slip, walk east up grand King Street, the city's main drag, to leafy **King's Square** ❻, laid out in 1785 and named for George III. At its heart is the **King Edward VII Memorial Bandstand**, a beloved city landmark, its copper roof and delicate

City Market   *The bandstand in King's Square*

filigree metal framework completed in 1908 – free concerts are often held here in the summer months. The fountain underneath dates back to 1851. Note the **"Loyalist Cross"** on the east side of the square, raised in 1934 to commemorate the Loyalists who fled here after the American Revolution, and the nearby **War Memorial**, sculpted by Alfred Howell in 1925. On the west side stands a statue of **Sir Samuel Leonard Tilley** (1818–1896), former Lieutenant Governor of New Brunswick, and a Father of Confederation.

CITY MARKET

On the northwest side of King's Square lies the cheery **City Market** ❼ (47 Charlotte St; http://sjcitymarket.ca; Mon–Fri 7.30am–6pm, Sat 7.30am–5pm), in operation since 1876 (it narrowly escaped the great fire the following year) and a great spot for lunch (see ❷). The market is heaped with fresh fruits and the characteristic foods of New Brunswick – fiddleheads, a succulent fern tip that tastes rather like asparagus, and dulse, dried seaweed from Grand Manan Island sold by **Slocum & Ferris** (https://slocumandferris.com), here since 1895.

The **City Market Bell**, located over the Deputy Market Clerk's office, is still rung every day to mark the opening and closing of the market.

LOYALIST HOUSE

After lunch stroll north along Charlotte Street, then one block west along Union Street to the white clapboard **Loyalist House** ❽ (120 Union St; https://loyalisthouse.com; mid-May to Oct Mon–Sat 10am–5pm; $5). Completed in 1817 for merchant David Merritt – who fled colonial Rye in New York after the American Revolution – it boasts an attractive Georgian interior and is one of the oldest homes in the city.

Despite arriving here with little money, Merritt became a wealthy shopkeeper. Thanks to Merritt's ancestors, who lived here until 1958 and never threw anything away, it's kitted out with a remarkable ensemble of original furnishings. Enthusiastic guides bring these pieces to life and provide a good introduction to the Loyalist story; favourites include the disguised water closet, a clock made in London around 1780 and a bed once slept in by the future Edward VII.

REVERSING FALLS RAPIDS

Like just about everywhere else on the shores of the Bay of Fundy, Saint John is proud of its explosive tides. What you have here are the impressive **Reversing Falls Rapids**, created by a sharp bend in the St John River about 3km southwest of Loyalist House.

Reversing Falls from Skywalk Saint John

If the weather is fine it's a pleasant walk via the Harbour Passage Trail from the western end of Union Street, along the riverside. The trail ends at a viewing station high above the rapids at the bridge on Rte-100. On the other side of the bridge you'll find **Reversing Falls Rapids Visitor Center** ❾ (200 Bridge Rd; https://skywalksaintjohn.com; late May to Oct daily 9am–sunset; Nov to late May Wed–Sun 11am–sunset; $15; $7 off-season), containing the Rapids Gift Shop, Reversing Falls Restaurant and Skywalk Saint John, which includes a 12-minute film that explains the falls phenomenon, and a stainless steel and glass platform that juts out from the cliff over the river.

At low tide, the rapids flow quite normally, but the incoming tide forces them into reverse, causing a brief period of equilibrium when the surface of the water is totally calm, before a churning, often tumultuous, surge upstream (see the visitor centre website for tide times). Several other vantage points are posted along the river, with **Fallsview Park** ❿ (best reached by taxi or car) the closest to the fiercest cascades.

You can also zipline along the riverbank and over the local seals with **Saint John Adventures** at 50 Fallsview Ave (http://saintjohnadventures.ca; June to late Oct;). This is a fantastic experience that shoudn't be missed. End the day with an evening at the **Water Street Dinner Theater** (http://waterstreetdinnertheatre.com), which offers tasty meals and a show with lots of laughs (usually 6.30–10pm).

Food and Drink

❶ ART WAREHOUSE

120 Prince William St; www.theartwarehousesj.com; tel: 506-608 3952; Sun–Thu 9am–4pm, Sun Fri and Sat 9am–10pm; $

High quality café decorated with murals and local art, serving excellent coffee from Nova Scotia's fair trade Just Us (including iced lattes and oat milk options), as well as tasty baked goods (blueberry lemon tarts), and even wine and beer.

❷ CITY MARKET

47 Charlotte St; http://sjcitymarket.ca; tel: 506-658 2820; Mon–Fri 7.30am–6pm, Sat 7.30am–5pm; $

Enticing food stalls here include the aromatic meat kebabs at Shawarma Hut, fabulous salads at Wild Carrot Café (www.wildcarrotcafe.ca), Jeremiah's Deli (www.jeremiahsdeli.ca) sandwiches and "Dave's Famous Chili" at Slocum & Ferris. There's also Billy's Seafood (https://billysseafood.com), a more formal restaurant serving up fresh seafood such as lobster by the pound, clams, beer battered haddock and chips and crab cakes.

Fundy coastline from along the Fundy footpath

THE FUNDY COASTAL DRIVE

Some of the most alluring scenery in the Maritimes can be found along New Brunswick's Fundy Coast, a wild and mostly untouched region of rugged headlands, crumbling cliffs and dense, fog–bound forests trailing into the sea.

DISTANCE: 260km
TIME: 3 days
START: Saint John
END: Moncton
POINTS TO NOTE: As with the rest of the Maritimes, most sights along the Fundy Coast are only open fully in the summer months (June to September). Indeed, the Fundy coast is a popular holiday spot in the summer, so book accommodation in advance (see page 111). This route has been designed as a road-trip: you'll need a car to make the most of the area, as there is no public transport to either St Martins or Fundy National Park. Ongoing COVID-19 restrictions may impact the opening times listed below – check websites to confirm if you plan to visit a specific sight.

The most enticing section of New Brunswick's Bay of Fundy coastline lies between Moncton and Saint John, taking in the scenic Fundy Trail Parkway and Fundy National Park. The main sights are easily accessed via routes 114 and 111, collectively dubbed the Fundy Coastal Drive.

The Bay of Fundy itself is known principally for its incredible tides, which rise and fall as much as 16.3 metres each day – towards the northern end of the bay, the effect can be mesmerizing, as mud-bound harbours fill with swirling water in a matter of hours, and rivers channel tidal bores far inland. Be prepared for patches of pea-soup fog: the Bay of Fundy is notoriously prone to them.

ST MARTINS

Start your journey at the former shipbuilding village of **St Martins ❶**, which winds along the Bay of Fundy shoreline about 40km to the east of Saint John. The pretty ensemble of neat gardens and clapboard houses culminates (after 3km) at the harbour, a compact affair of lobster pots and skiffs set within a ring of hills. Be sure to get a photo of the twin covered bridges over the Irish River (the Vaughan Creek Bridge was built in 1935; upriver is the Hardscrabble Bridge of 1946) along with the lighthouse (the information centre),

Vaughan Creek Bridge

built in 1983 and actually a replica of the old Quaco Head Lighthouse. History buffs may want to stop in at the tiny **Quaco Museum**, just before the harbour (236 Main St; https://quaco.ca; late June to Aug Tue–Sat 10am–5pm; Sept to mid-Nov Tue–Sat 10am–4.30pm; free, donation requested). The museum chronicles the surprisingly rich history of St Martins.

FUNDY TRAIL PARKWAY

From St Martin's harbour it's 8km east along Big Salmon River Road to the **Fundy Trail Parkway** ❷ (Western Entrance; https://fundytrailparkway.

com; daily: mid May to late June and early Sept to mid-Oct 9am–5pm; late June to late Aug 8am–8pm; late Aug to early Sept 9am–7pm; $10), one of the province's most magical destinations. The 30km parkway threads past craggy headlands, dense forest and stupendous viewpoints at almost every turn; you might see moose, porcupine and deer along the way. The road is also shadowed by a multi-use trail offering fine and comparatively easy hiking and biking, as well as access to several gorgeous beaches and falls. Aim to spend the best part of the day here (bring a picnic).

Highlights include the Fox Rock Look-

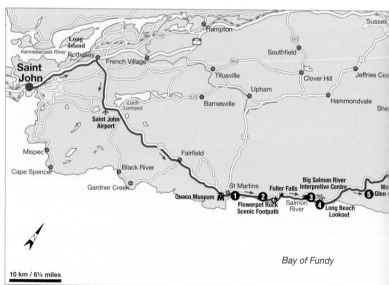

Fundy Trail Parkway   *Exploring the coast near St Martins*

out just beyond the entrance, and the nearby Fownes Head Lookout where you can hike down the **Flowerpot Rock Scenic Footpath**. Continue driving the parkway to **Fuller Falls**, then on to the **Big Salmon River Interpretive Centre ❸**. The nearby **Cookhouse** offers more exhibits on the lumber industry. From the Interpretive Centre, you can stroll down the hillside and cross the suspension bridge to the river below before driving on to **Long Beach Lookout** with spectacular views across Tufts' Point. From here you can lounge on **Long Beach ❹**, or hike up to **Long Beach Brook Falls**. After this the parkway starts to snake inland towards

the McCumber Brook/Walton Glen Gorge/Falls area, accessible from Parking Lot 15 (near the eastern entrance). From here a 1.1km (one-way) trail runs to an overlook across stunning **Walton Glen Gorge ❺**, dubbed the "Grand Canyon of New Brunswick". By the end of 2021 you should be able to drive from here direct to Alma. For accommodation in Alma, see page 111 – reserve two nights here.

FUNDY NATIONAL PARK

Devote the whole of day two to exploring **Fundy National Park ❻** (mid-May

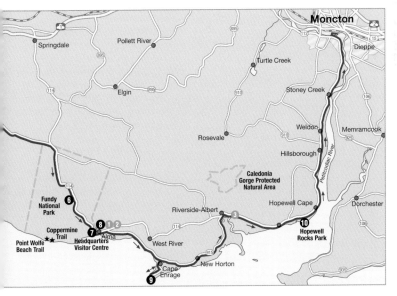

Hiking in Fundy National Park

to mid-Oct daily 8am–6pm $7.90, free at other times). Bisected by Rte-114, Fundy National Park encompasses a short stretch of the Bay of Fundy's pristine shoreline, all jagged cliffs and tidal mudflats, and the forested hills, lakes and river valleys of the central plateau behind. This varied scenery is crossed by more than 100km of hiking trails, mostly short and easy walks taking no more than three hours to complete. The shady **Point Wolfe Beach Trail** is a moderately steep, 600m hike down from the spruce woodlands above the bay to the grey-sand beach below (15min). Of equal appeal is the 4.4km loop of the **Coppermine Trail** (1hr 30min–2hr), which meanders through the forests with awe-inspiring views out along the seashore. All the park's trails are described on a free map issued on arrival at either of the two Rte-114 entrance kiosks.

Start by stopping by the **Headquar-ters Visitor Centre** ❼ on Rte-114 just beyond the entrance (www.pc.gc.ca/en/pn-np/nb/fundy; late Jan to late May Wed and Thu 8.30am–4.15pm Fri–Tue 10am–5.45pm; late May to late June daily 8am–6.45pm; late June to early Sept daily 8am–9.45pm, early Sept to late Oct daily 8am–7.45pm). Inside are displays on local flora and fauna, as well as information on guided walks and detailed hiking maps.

Alma

Alma ❽ is a sleepy little village just across the Salmon River from the east entrance to the national park, and makes a good overnight base. The highlight here is food – the village contains three lobster pounds that sell the local Fundy Bay variety. Most shops also sell scallops, smoked salmon, oysters and fresh fish, ideal for picnics. Otherwise, try a cooked lobster at **Alma Lobster Shop** (see ❶), the sticky buns at **Kelly's Bake Shop**, or the coffee at **Buddha Bear Coffee Roasters and Café** (see ❷).

CAPE ENRAGE

Start day three with the 20km drive from Alma along the coast to **Cape Enrage** ❾ (www.capeenrage.ca/en; daily: late May to late June and Sept 9.30am–5pm; late June to Aug 9am–6pm; $6; family $20), 6.5km down a side road off Rte-915. The red and white Cape Enrage lighthouse of 1870 is still glued to a great shank of rock soaring high above

The Fundy Footpath

Experienced hikers can tackle the 49.3km between Fundy National Park and the Fundy Trail Parkway via the spectacular coastal Fundy Footpath (https://fundyhikingtrails.com), accessible from the end of Goose River Path (7.9km; 2hr 30min) from Point Wolfe in Fundy National Park. The challenging trail ends near the Big Salmon River Interpretive Centre on the Parkway. Most people take four or five days and camp along the way.

Hopewell Rocks

the Bay of Fundy here. There's a wooden walkway up to the foot of the lighthouse, a path down to the beach, and the old keeper's house has been converted into the **Gallery at the Cape** and **Cape House Restaurant**. In the summer there's a programme of adventure sports, principally rappelling ($95) and zip-lining (three runs; $50).

HOPEWELL ROCKS

From Cape Enrage, it's 42km northeast along the Fundy shore to the captivating shoreline of **Hopewell Cape**, contained within the privately managed **Hopewell Rocks Park** ⑩ (https://thehopewell rocks.ca/index.php/en/home; daily: mid-May to late June and early Sept to mid-Oct 8am–5pm; late June to late Aug 8am–8pm; late Aug to early Sept 8am–7pm; $15). A recommended option for lunch on the way is **Broadleaf Ranch** (see ③), though the canteen style **High Tide Café** at Hopewell itself is usually fine. There's an interpretive centre at the park's upper section, but head down the 828m footpath to the lower section to the gnarled red-sandstone pinnacles known as the Flowerpot Rocks (golf carts shuttle back and forth for $2 one way). Steps lead down to the beach and you can safely walk round the rocks two to three hours either side of low tide, or paddle round them at high tide by taking a guided tour by kayak (www.baymountadventures. com; June–Sept; from $82;). Your ticket is valid for two days. From Hopewell it's a short 38km drive northwest to along the Petitcodiac River to Moncton on Rte-114.

Food and Drink

① ALMA LOBSTER SHOP
36 Shore Lane, off Foster Rd, Alma; www.thankfultoo.com/alma; tel: 506-887 1987; daily 11am–9pm; $$
Overlooking the water, this shop sells live (by the pound, market price) and cooked lobsters (around $2–3 more); buy one to eat on the picnic tables outside (they offer lobster rolls and complete lobster dinners). Daily 11am–9pm.

② BUDDHA BEAR COFFEE ROASTER
8576 Main St, Alma; www.facebook.com/ buddhabearcafe; tel: 506-887 1999; Wed and Thu 4–9pm, Fri 1–9pm, Sat noon–10pm, Sun noon–8pm; $
Old church artfully converted into this excellent café, which shares the space with Holy Whale Brewery. Sip espresso, tea hot chocolate or craft beers on the patio.

③ BROADLEAF RANCH
5526 Rte-114, Hopewell Hill; https://broadleafranch.ca; tel: 506-882 2349; mid-May to early Oct daily 8am–9pm; open limited hours thereafter; $$
This rustic hotel boasts an excellent restaurant serving breakfast, lunch and dinner – the Sunday brunch (10am–2pm; $15) is justly popular. Try local fiddleheads in a hot cheesy citrus dip.

DIRECTORY

Hand-picked hotels and restaurants to suit all budgets and tastes, organised by area, plus select nightlife listings and an overview of the best books and films to give you a flavour of the region.

Room at the Sheraton Hotel Newfoundland

ACCOMMODATION

Whilst the major cities and tourist areas of Nova Scotia, New Brunswick and PEI offer plenty of accommodation, choices can dwindle dramatically when travelling through the more rural regions of the Maritimes. This is doubly true of Newfoundland and especially Labrador – it's advisable to book all accommodation as far in advance as possible. In general, chain motels are far scarcer than in provinces further west. Hotels and even motels tend to be on the pricey side in the peak summer months, and many hotels and B&Bs close completely for the coldest half of the year. Camping is popular in national parks in the summer, and there are a handful of hostels in the bigger cities, but true budget options – anything under $100 – are rare throughout the region.

Note also that harmonized sales tax (HST) is high out here. On the plus side are family-owned hotels and B&Bs offering exceptional friendly service and home-cooked breakfasts, often housed in historic 19th-century properties with a ton of character.

Price for a standard double room for one night in high season:
$ = below $100
$$ = $100–150
$$$ = $151–200
$$$$ = above $200

Newfoundland: St John's

HI St John's City Hostel
8 Gower St; tel: 709-754 4789, www.hihostels.ca; $
Solid backpacker option offering dorms and private rooms, all within stumbling distance of George Street. You get lockers, a decent shared kitchen, free wi-fi (use of computers) and very laidback staff.

Ryan Mansion
21 Rennies Mill Rd; tel: 709-753 7926; http://ryanmansion.com; $$$$
Lavishly maintained 1911 Edwardian property, with utterly luxurious suites (home to Prince Charles and Camilla in 2009); bathrooms come with steam rooms, heated marble floors, jacuzzis and Victorian tubs, while the beds are comfortable hardwood four-posters.

Sheraton Hotel Newfoundland
115 Cavendish Square; tel: 709-726 4980; www.marriott.com; $$$
The city's most famous hotel, whose earliest incarnation dates back to 1926. All the rooms are kitted out in top-whack chain style and most have great views over the harbour. Indoor pool and fitness facilities included.

Newfoundland: The Irish Loop

Dunne's Bed & Breakfast
Hwy-10, Ferryland; tel: 709-432 2155;

Room at the Fogo Island Inn

https://dunnesbnb.com; $$
Friendly digs managed by Charlie and Maxine Dunne, who offer four ocean front rooms, wi-fi, complimentary tea and coffee and a font of local knowledge (plus their own CD of traditional Irish/Newfoundland music). Cash, travellers cheque or e-transfer only.

Edge of the Avalon Inn

113 Coarse Hill Rd, Trepassey; tel: 709-438 2934; www.edgeoftheavaloninn.com; $$
Beautiful property with friendly owners, suites (with soaker tubs) and rooms blending red-brick, wood and modern appliances, plus ocean-view cottages (3–4 bedrooms), bar and restaurant on site – often with live music. Continental breakfast included.

Newfoundland: The Baccalieu Trail

Cupids Haven B&B

169 Burnt Head Rd, Cupids; tel: 729-528 1555; http://cupidshaven.ca; $$
Superb accommodation in a beautifully converted Anglican chapel built in 1910; rooms feature original Gothic windows and wooden fittings. The on-site Tea Room serves great pots of tea, pan-fried cod and classic treats such as toutons (pancakes) with molasses.

Grates Cove Studio

Main Road, Grates Cove; tel: 709-587 3880; www.gratescovestudios.ca; $$
This art studio and restaurant offers cosy rooms in two adjacent properties;

Harbour House (open year-round), with three private en-suite rooms with fully equipped shared kitchen, patio and ocean views; and Snug Harbour, which offers three rooms with shared bath ($185).

Newfoundland: Bonavista Peninsula

Artisan Inn

57 High St, Trinity; tel: 709-464 3377; www.trinityvacations.com; $$$
This "diffused hotel" offers accommodation in several Victorian buildings, foremost of which is the gorgeous 1840s Campbell House. It has two double rooms, both en suite. Register first at the *Twine Loft*, where breakfast is included.

Newfoundland: Kittiwake Coast

Fogo Island Inn

210 Main Rd (Hwy-334), Joe Batt's Arm, Fogo Island; tel: 709-658 3444; https://fogoislandinn.ca; $$$$
The culmination of Zita Cobb's vision for the island, this five-star, stilt-raised edifice dominates the horizon, featuring floor-to-ceiling windows, ocean views, infinity pool and luxurious contemporary rooms. It's a spectacular but exclusive experience, with rooms priced accordingly (from $1975). Full board only.

Toulinguet Inn

56 Main St, Twillingate; tel: 709-884 2080, www.toulinguetinn.com; $$

The Waverley

Cosy, en-suite rooms down on the waterfront, in a 1920s saltbox, with balconies overlooking Twillingate harbour and continental style breakfast served in room. You can also rent two complete cottages. Open Mid-May to mid-Oct.

Newfoundland: Gros Morne National Park

Bonne Bay Inn

145 Main Rd, Woody Point; tel: 709-453 2223; https://woodypointmagic.com/bonne-bay-inn; $$$

This modern, cosy hotel offers sensational views across the bay, 10 comfy en-suite bedrooms with ocean views (and locally made quilts), and the congenial *Elements Pub* and *Blue Ocean Dining Room*. Breakfast is included. Open May to early Oct.

Ocean View Hotel

38–42 Main St, Rocky Harbour; tel: 709-458 2730; https://theoceanview.ca; $$$

Fabulous location in the heart of Rocky Harbour, overlooking the waterfront, with 53 modern a/c rooms with cable TV and a decent restaurant with sea views. Usually open mid-Apr to mid-Dec.

Newfoundland: Viking Trail

Crows Nest Inn

1 Spruce Lane, St Anthony; tel: 709-454 3402; http://crowsnestinn.ca; $$

For comfortable accommodation, try this sensitively renovated B&B, with eight spacious rooms equipped with cable TV and wi-fi, most offering fine views of St Anthony's harbour. Usually open year-round.

Jenny's Runestone House

Main Rd, Hay Cove (L'Anse aux Meadows); tel: 709-623 2811; www.jennysrunestonehouse.ca; $$$

Exceptionally friendly accommodations with Ontario transplants Jenny and David, with four cosy rooms (wi-fi but no TV) offering fabulous ocean views, within walking distance of Norstead. Full breakfast included. Open year-round.

Labrador: Trans-Labrador Highway

Northern Light Inn

58 Main St (rte-510), L'Anse au Clair; tel: 709-931 2332; www.northernlightinn.com; $$

A modern, but rather basic, motel with clean rooms, a/c, cable TV, free wi-fi and the most popular food options in town. It also rents five two-bedroom cottages with full kitchens. Open year-round.

Riverlodge Hotel

6163 Main Rd (Rte-510), Mary's Harbour; tel: 709-921 6948, http://riverlodgehotel.ca; $$

Stay and eat at the comfortable hotel (with satellite TV) overlooking the river, where locals cook up hearty meals in the restaurant. *Old Pete's Pub*, also on the premises, is a good place to share stories with fellow travellers and locals.

Gisele's Inn

Royal Inn

5 Royal St, Happy Valley-Goose Bay; tel: 709-896 2456, http://royalinnandsuites. ca; $$

This centrally located, plush motel-like option is the best value in town; continental breakfast is included, rooms are new and comfy and it has self-service laundry and decent satellite TV. It's popular and can get very busy.

Nova Scotia: Halifax

Cambridge Suites Hotel

1583 Brunswick St; tel: 902-420 0555, www.cambridgesuiteshalifax.com; $$$

Large, luxurious hotel that offers spacious but affordable suites and studios, all decked out in swish, contemporary style; most rooms have superb views of the waterfront. Breakfast included.

The Waverley

1266 Barrington St; tel: 902-423 9346, http://waverleyinn.com; $$

Elegant Victorian mansion, with 30 en-suite a/c rooms, sympathetically refurbished with splendid period furnishings. Oscar Wilde stayed here on his 1882 North American lecture tour. Rates include breakfast and parking.

Halifax Backpackers Hostel

2193 Gottingen St, North End; tel: 902-431 3170, http://halifaxbackpackers.com; $

These spacious six-bed dorms are the best deal in the city. The café downstairs offers light meals, the shared kitchen is big and the owners invite all

guests to a barbecue every Friday. Parking is $5/day.

Nova Scotia: Cape Breton Island

Auberge Gisele's Inn

387 Shore Rd, Baddeck; tel: 902-295 2849, https://giseles.com; $$

Large, motel-like place overlooking Bras d'Or Lake, with commodious bedrooms decked out in floral, modern style and an excellent dining room. The deluxe rooms have fireplaces. Open May to late Oct.

Keltic Lodge Resort & Spa

383 Keltic Inn Rd, Ingonish Beach; tel: 902-285 2880, www.kelticlodge.ca; $$$$

Perched high above the cliffs amid immaculate gardens on Middle Head; features and facilities include beaches, restaurants, tennis courts and kayaks. You can stay in the main lodge, a handsome Edwardian mansion, or the modern inn, but the cottages are perhaps more enjoyable. Open Mid-May to mid-Oct.

MacDonald's Motel

5 Bay St Lawrence Rd, Cape North; tel: 902-383 2054; www.macdonaldsmotel. ca; $$

This handy motel has been open since 1939, offering ageing but exceptionally cheap rooms (with satellite TV and free wi-fi) at the Cape North village crossroads. Open Mid-May to mid-Oct.

The Great George

Hillsdale House Inn

519 St George St, Annapolis Royal; tel: 902-532 2345; www.hillsdalehouseinn.ca; $$
The best accommodation options in Annapolis Royal are its B&Bs, and this is one of the top choices, an elegant villa of 1859 with full country-style breakfast and 15 elegant rooms enhanced with antiques.

Jeremy's Bay Campground

Kejimkujik National Park; tel: 877-737 3783; https://reservation.pc.gc.ca; $
This large campground, some 10km from the main Kejimkujik entrance, offers sites with electricity, un-serviced sites, clean washrooms, hot showers and wi-fi (services May–Oct only). There are also posher oTENTik cabins (from $122), and rustic cabins ($102).

Kaulbach House

75 Pelham St, Lunenburg; tel: 902-634 8818; www.kaulbachhouse.com; $$$
One of the best preserved of Lunenburg's Victorian mansions, this comfortable inn, with its brightly painted exterior, has seven well-appointed guest rooms, most with sea views and all decorated in an attractive period style. The creative European breakfasts are delicious.

Charlottetown Backpackers Inn

60 Hillsborough St; tel: 902-367 5749; www.charlottetownbackpackers.com; $
Excellent HI-affiliated hostel with dorms and a few cheap private rooms in a renovated, three-storey house. There's a pool table, free parking and breakfast included, right in the heart of downtown. Open May to early Oct.

The Great George

58 Great George St; tel: 902-892 0606, https://thegreatgeorge.com; $$$$
Bang in the centre of town, opposite St Dunstan's, a row of 15 old timber houses has been carefully renovated to hold this immaculate and atmospheric hotel. All the rooms are comfortable and tastefully decorated – the most appealing overlook the church. A continental breakfast is included.

Shipwright Inn

51 Fitzroy St; tel: 902-368 1905, http://shipwrightinn.com; $$$
Crammed with antiques, this rambling 1865 timber mansion (with a more recent extension) has nine individually decorated guest rooms. Very appealing – especially with its thoughtful additions (like popcorn, afternoon tea and muffins, videos and CDs), and its superlative breakfasts.

FarmHouse Inn PEI

6123 Rte-13, New Glasgow; tel: 902-360 3600; www.farmhouseinnpei.com; $$$
Charming accommodation with rooms in the main farmhouse, Blueberry Hill cottage, and three cottage suites in

West Point Lighthouse Inn

"The Coop", all with free wi-fi and cable TV (full gourmet breakfast included for guests in the main farmhouse only).

Orient Hotel Bed and Breakfast
34 Main St, Victoria; tel: 800-565 6743; www.theorienthotel.com; $$
Historic hotel with heaps of character, established back in 1900, with comfy queen rooms, one- or two-bedroom suites. All have bathooms, cable TV and free wi-fi. Full breakfast included.

West Point Lighthouse Inn
364 Cedar Dunes Park Rd, O'Leary; tel: 902-859 3605; https://westpointharmony. ca; $$$
Stay in this remote lighthouse, lulled to sleep by the sound of crashing waves: The Tower Room is located on the second floor of the lighthouse, while the seaside rooms next to the lighthouse come with a walk-out deck overlooking the Northumberland Strait.

New Brunswick: Saint John

A Tanner's Home Inn
190 King St East; tel: 506-634 8917; www.tannershomeinn.com; $$
Just a short stroll from the city centre, this beautiful old house has five charming bedrooms decked out in Victorian period style. Breakfast, satellite TV and off-street parking included.

Chipman Hill Suites
9 Chipman Hill; tel: 506-693 1171; https://chipmanhill.com; $$

Centrally located suites in nine historic properties, all with fully equipped kitchenettes or kitchens and cable TV (all buildings have laundries), and all within a 5–10 minute walk of the Uptown's restaurants and bars – a fabulous deal.

Mahogany Manor B&B
220 Germain St; tel: 506-636 8000; www.bb canada.com/mahoganymanorbnb; $$
This is the pick of Uptown's B&Bs, with six en-suite guest rooms in an elegant Edwardian villa. Located in a quiet, leafy part of town, a10min walk southeast of Market Slip. Free parking.

New Brunswick: Fundy Coastal Drive

Parkland Village Inn
8601 Main St (Hwy-114), Alma; tel: 506-887 2313, www.parklandvillageinn.com; $$
This is a standard two-storey, motel-like option on the main street, with breakfast included Apr–June and Sept–Oct. The ageing rooms are a little old-fashioned but come with cable TV – the deluxe rooms have ocean views. Open Apr–Nov only.

Residence Inn by Marriott Moncton
600 Main St, Moncton; tel: 506-854 7100; www.marriott.com; $$
One of the newer hotels in Moncton is also one of the best, and the most centrally located, steps from Bore Park. Each spacious suite comes with sitting area, kitchen and flat-screen TV. Decent Pool and gym; parking $15/day.

Fish and chips in Newfoundland

RESTAURANTS

In the biggest cities of Canada's Atlantic provinces – Halifax, Saint John, Moncton and St John's – there's a plethora of international and speciality restaurants, with most global cuisines and chains represented. Beyond these cities, however, choices can narrow dramatically, within many small towns featuring just one or two places to eat in total, often family-run cafés and diners.

The region excels in fresh seafood. Fish and chips is big in all four provinces, along with fresh cod, haddock, salmon, shrimp, mussels, scallops, clams and lobster. No-frills lobster shacks – selling fresh, live lobsters, as well as freshly boiled lobsters – are common in the Maritimes, with Prince Edward Island especially known for its "lobster suppers" served in communal halls as part of gut-busting set menus.

Newfoundland is sprinkled with locally celebrated fish and chip shops, though in many villages and towns the local inn doubles as a restaurant. Another phenomenon – in a province where long drives are common – are the Big Stop diners at Irving gas stations (and many others), which here often serve as the top local restaurants, run by locals who cook classic Newfoundland food in addition to fast-food staples. Few restaurants in any of the four provinces beyond major cities open year-round; most fully open May or June through to September or October, then close or open with limited hours thereafter.

Newfoundland: St John's

Basho

283 Duckworth St; tel: 709-576 4600; www.bashorestaurant.com; Mon–Sat 6–11pm; $$$

Shrine to Japanese fusion cuisine by Tak Ishiwata, a student of New York-based maestro Nobu Matsuhisa. The food is exceptional: think pan-seared caribou steak, sushi rolls and iceberg Martinis made with real chunks of Greenland bergs.

Ches's Fish & Chips

9 Freshwater Rd; tel: 709-726 2373; www.chessfishandchips.ca; Mon–Thu and Sun 9am–2am, Fri and Sat 9am–3am; $

Legendary fish and chips since 1951 ("chesses"), with several locations in the city (Freshwater is closest to downtown); the main event is two pieces of crisp cod served with hand-cut chips,

> Throughout this book, price guide for a two-course meal for one with an alcoholic drink:
> $$$$ = over $75
> $$$ = $51–75
> $$ = $25–50
> $ = below $25

The Rocket and Water St in St Johns

though the menu also offers cod bites, chicken wings, burgers and shellfish.

Pi

10 Kings Rd; tel: 709-726 2000; https://pinl.ca; Mon and Wed–Sat noon–3pm and 5–9pm, Sun 4–9pm; $$
Best pizza in Newfoundland, thin-crusted delights made with vegan-friendly dough and innovative toppings; the "pi" offers shaved steak, roasted red peppers, mushrooms, avocado slices and leeks.

Rocket Bakery & Fresh Food

272 Water St; tel: 709-738 2011; https://rocketfood.ca; Mon–Fri 7.30am–10pm, Sat 8am–10pm, Sun 8am–6pm; $
Café and bakery selling exquisite pain au chocolat, partridgeberry macaroons, croissants, fresh bread, salads, fish cakes and filling sandwiches. Seating area or takeaway.

Newfoundland

Big Stop

62 Trans-Canada Hwy, Deer Lake; tel: 709-635 2130; daily 8am–8pm; $
For meals in Deer Lake, most travellers opt for this convenient option, at the Irving gas station. It serves a full menu of classic dishes (turkey dinners, grilled salmon), the obligatory fish and chips and hefty lemon meringue pies, plus superb homemade Newfoundland dishes not on the standard menu.

The Black Spruce

7 Beach Rd, Neddies Harbour, Norris Point (Gros Morne); tel: 709-458 3089; https://theblackspruce.ca; Tue–Sun 5–9pm; $$$
This hotel restaurant serves superb gourmet dinners, featuring such delights as slow roasted sweet potato soup, Newfoundland mussels, rack of lamb and local desserts like steamed carrot pudding.

Juniper Kitchen & Bistro

48 High St, Grand Falls-Windsor; tel: 709-393 3663; daily 11.30am–2pm and 5–9pm; $$
The best restaurant in Grand Falls – you won't find better quality: the seafood chowder and Atlantic salmon fillet are excellent, but it's always worth asking about the nightly specials. Lunch sandwiches and salads are much cheaper.

Newfound Sushi

117 Broadway, Corner Brook; tel: 709-634 6666, https://newfoundsushi.com; Tue–Sat 4–9.30pm; $$
Small (seven tables) but top-notch sushi restaurant (think Atlantic salmon, snow crab, shrimp and smoked Arctic char) from Kevin Vincent, the only sushi place in NL outside St John's, with salads, stir-fries and grilled seafood also on the menu.

Old Loft Restaurant

8 Water St, Bonne Bay (Woody Point); tel: 709-453 2294; http://the-old-loft.edan.io; late May to Sept daily 11am–9pm; $$
Fine dining in the southern section of Gros Morne National Park, where tasty seafood (scallops wrapped in bacon, pan-fried cod, chowder, fish cakes) and

King Of Donair

traditional island dishes (cod cheeks) are served up in a 1936 clapboard fishing loft near the water.

Labrador: Trans-Labrador Highway

Mariner's Galley

25 Loring Drive, Happy Valley-Goose Bay; tel: 709-896 9301; daily 6am–9pm; $$
Excellent option for breakfast, lunch and dinner, specializing in steaks and fine seafood; most popular joint for out-of-towners. The nautical theme is enhanced by the wooden ship centrepiece.

Maxwells & Bentley's

97 Hamilton River Rd, Happy Valley-Goose Bay; tel: 709-896 3565; www.maxwellsandbentleys.ca; Mon–Sat 11am–9.30pm; $$
Located right on the waterfront, Bentley's restaurant is the main spot for a meal and night out, featuring a sports bar showing all the big events. Lunch specials are also good, as well as pastas, salmon, cod dishes, steaks and grills. The other side of the building morphs into Maxwell's nightclub Thu–Sat nights.

Nova Scotia: Halifax

Bluenose II

1824 Hollis St; tel: 902-425 5092; https://bluenoseii.ca; daily 8am–9pm; $$
An institution since 1964, this diner serves filling and fairly tasty meals (including breakfasts). Seafood, in various guises, is the real speciality, along with Greek dishes (lamb chops, souvlaki),

excellent burgers and the signature rice pudding.

Five Fishermen

1740 Argyle St; tel: 902-422 4421; www.fivefishermen.com; daily 5–10pm; $$$
One of Halifax's best restaurants, where the house speciality is seafood (and Alberta Angus beef). It's expensive, but the food is exceptional and the all-you-can-eat mussel bar is included in the price of any main dish. The restaurant is on the first floor of a gorgeous 1816 building and its cosy interior, with its booths and stained glass, is decked out in antique nautical style.

King of Donair

6420 Quinpool Rd; tel: 902-421 0000; www.kingofdonair.ca; Mon–Wed and Sun 10am–1am, Thu–Sat 10am–3am; $
The mini-chain that claims to have started the "donair" kebab craze in Halifax back in 1973 still knocks out some of the best, as well as donair pizza. Legend has it that Greek founder Peter Gamoulakos replaced the traditional lamb kebab with spiced ground beef, and the tzatziki with a sweet sauce, thus creating the "donair", which has cult status in Halifax.

Steve-o-Reno's

1536 Brunswick St, just off Spring Garden Rd; tel: 902-429 3034; www.steveorenos.com; Mon–Fri 7am–5pm, Sat 7.30am–5pm, Sun 7.30am–4pm (seasonal hours); $
New Age-ish café-bar with bohemian decor and laidback vibes. The breakfasts

are tip-top, with a bewildering range of coffees from local roasters North Mountain Fine Coffees.

Nova Scotia: Cape Breton Island

Baddeck Lobster Suppers

17 Ross St, Baddeck; tel: 902-295 3307; www.baddecklobstersuppers.ca; early June to mid-Oct daily 4–9pm; $$$

Located inside the converted 19th-century Armoury, overlooking Bras d'Or Lake, this place excels in "hot planked" smoked salmon, as well as its signature fresh lobster suppers (with unlimited chowder, fresh mussels, rolls, biscuits, salads and desserts).

Nova Scotia: South Shore and the Annapolis Valley

Antonio's

9066 Hwy-101, Brighton (Scotia Bay Motel); tel: 902-245 5698; mid-June to late Sept Mon–Fri 4–9pm, Sat and Sun noon–9pm; $$

This no-frills diner just outside Digby has garnered a cult following in the province for its sumptuous (English-style) haddock and chips, fresh scallops, and clams, as well as its decent pastas and pizzas.

Fundy Restaurant

34 Water St, Digby; tel: 902-245 4950, www.fundyrestaurant.com; Sun–Wed 11am–8pm, Thu–Sun 11am–8.30pm; $$

Digby's delicious scallops (seasonal prices) are the main event here, but fish and chips, fried clams and a display of rare blue lobsters (live) are also a major plus.

The Half Shell

108 Montague St, Lunenburg; tel: 902-634 8503; www.halfshelloysterbar.com; late May to Sept daily noon–9pm (July and Aug noon–midnight); $$

High-quality seafood served on an outdoor deck with fabulous views – everything from steamed mussels and fresh oysters, to rich chowder and scallop carbonara. Closes if it rains or is too cold.

Knot Pub

4 Dufferin St, Lunenburg; tel: 902-634 3334; www.theknotpub.ca; Mon–Thu 10am–midnight, Fri and Sat 10am–1am, Sun noon–midnight; $$

Quirky sea shanty-esque bar and restaurant with cosy oak and brass interior serving delicious potato skins, fish chowder, seafood (fish and chips, pan-fried scallops, haddock, fish cakes) and salads.

PEI: Charlottetown

Cedar's Eatery

181 Great George St; tel: 902-892 7377; www.cedarseatery.ca; Mon–Thu 11am–9pm, Fri and Sat 11am–10pm; $$

Charlottetown has had a relatively large Lebanese population since the 1880s, and this is one of their favourite haunts; think hummus, fragrant kafta and stuffed vine leaves.

Kettle Black

45 Queen St; tel: 902-370 0776; daily

Water Prince Corner Shop

8am–5pm; $

Hip café managed by a couple of Ottawa transplants, serving the best coffee (in real mugs) and desserts in town. They also do breakfast bagels and yoghurt bowls, sandwiches and wraps.

Sim's Corner Steakhouse & Oyster Bar

86 Queen St; tel: 902-894 7467; https://simscorner.ca; daily 11.30am–8pm (bar until 10pm); $$$

The town's top restaurant, with delectable local oysters, a huge wine list and prime Canadian aged steaks – try the secret pepper sauce. Features outdoor terrace and barbecues in summer.

Water Prince Corner Shop

141 Water St; tel: 902-368 3212; https://waterprincelobster.com; daily: May, June and Sept to Oct 10am–8pm; July and Aug 10am–10pm; Nov to mid-Dec noon–8pm; $

The lobster dinners and chowders here are perhaps the best on the island, but the scallop burger is superb too. You can also buy fresh lobsters to go. Moderately priced with mains from as little as $10.

PEI

FireWorks Feast

Inn at Bay Fortune, 758 Rte-310, Bay Fortune; tel: 902-687 3745; https://innatbay fortune.com/fireworks; late May to late Oct daily 5pm; $$$$

For a real treat, head to the innovative restaurant of chef Michael Smith, inter-nationally lauded for its eight-course set menus of organic and foraged local dishes, cooked over a wood-burning fire and served family style ("feasts" are $175/person, includes tips; drinks are extra).

Landmark Oyster House

12 Main St, Victoria; tel: 902-658 2286; www.landmarkoysterhouse.com; June–Sept daily 11am–4pm and 5–9pm (seasonal hours differ): $$

The focus here is on fresh PEI oysters ($2.50), but there's also a wonder-ful chowder, fish cakes, pastas, curry chicken salad, and a range of cocktails and speciality coffees.

The Lobster Shack

8 Main St, Souris; tel: 902-743 3347; https://colvillebayoysterco.com; mid-June to mid-Sept daily 10am–7pm; $

The retail outlet for Colville Bay Oyster Co, this small shack on the beach sells some of the island's best oysters, fresh from the bay, plus lobster rolls and fresh and cooked island lobster (take-out only – eat on the picnic tables on the board-walk).

Samuel's Coffee House

4 Queen St, Summerside; tel: 902-724 2300; https://samuelscoffeehouse.ca; Mon–Sat 7.30am–5pm, Sun 9am–4pm; $

Cosy café housed in the old Summerside Bank building (you can even sit in the old vault), serving superb coffee, pastries, Montréal-style bagels and breakfast

Pizza at the Pumphouse Brewery (see page 119)

"sammies" (stuffed with egg, spinach, cheese and tomato).

New Brunswick: Saint John

Church Street Steakhouse

10 Grannan St; tel: 506-648 2373; https://grannangroup.ca; Mon–Wed 11.30am–1am, Thu–Sat 11.30am–2am, Sun 10.30am–midnight; $$$
Best steaks in the city, using prime Angus beef, as well fish n' chips, bean burgers, poutine, fried chicken sandwiches and salads.

Grannan's Seafood Restaurant

Level 1, Market Square (on Market Slip); tel: 506-634 1555; https://grannangroup.ca; Mon–Thu 11.30am–11pm, Fri and Sat 11.30am–2am), Sun noon–10pm; $$$
This is a great option; the catch of the day and fresh lobster is a treat and you get everything from haddock and chips and mussels, to maritime fish pie and maple curry chicken pasta.

Tops Pizza Restaurant

215 Union St; tel: 506-634 0505; daily 7am–9pm; $
This old-school diner and local favourite knocks out decent pizzas but also great lasagne, coleslaw and home-made soups – you can have a filling lunch for under $10. Cash only.

New Brunswick: Fundy Coastal Drive

Coastal Tides

7 Beach St, St Martin's; tel: 506-833 1103; June–Sept Tue–Sat 11am–7pm, Sun 9am–6pm; Oct–Dec and Mar–May Fri 4–7pm, Sat 11am–7pm, Sun 9am–6pm); $$
Mingle with the locals over strong coffee at this friendly diner just off Main Street; it offers burgers, scallop and chips, lobster rolls, chowder and a small Chinese menu.

Fundy Take-Out Restaurant

21 Fundy View Drive, Alma; tel: 506-887 2261; May–Oct Mon–Thu 11am–7pm, Fri and Sat 11am–10pm, Sun 11am–7.30pm; $
Overlooking the Salmon River, this no-frills shack knocks out fried chicken, fish and chips, fried breaded clams and lobster rolls you can eat on picnic tables with poutine.

Kelly's Bake Shop

8587 Main St, Alma; tel: 506-887 2460; daily: May and June 10am–5pm, July and Aug 7am–6pm, Sept and Oct 8.30am–5pm; $
For something sweet, visit this lauded bakery (in business over 50 years), best known for its enormous, delicious sticky buns and array of tempting cakes.

Tides Restaurant

8601 Main St (Parkland Village Inn), Alma; tel: 506-887 2313; May–Oct daily 11am–7pm; Nov–Apr Thu–Sun 11am–7pm; $$
The best place for a sit-down meal in Alma; the seafood chowder is a worthy house special (there's also hickory smoked ribs, baby clam linguine and grilled New York sirloin) and the views of the bay are fabulous.

Beer garden on the Waterfront in Halifax

NIGHTLIFE

Nightlife in Atlantic Canada traditionally revolves around live music (usually local or Irish folk music) performed in pubs – this is especially true in Newfoundland and on Cape Breton Island (see page 71). However, in the bigger cities (especially Halifax) there's everything from classic old-time bars and hopping nightclubs, to sophisticated cocktail lounges and craft beer joints. In smaller towns the local hotel or diner often doubles as a bar or live venue, where local musicians are as likely to simply turn up and play as be booked in advance. The four provinces also boast a small but flourishing theatre scene, with shows and festivals especially lively in the summer months. The following listings are just a selection.

Bars and taprooms

Annapolis Brewing Company

302 St George St, Annapolis Royal, NS; tel: 902-286 2080; www.annapolisbrewing. com; Sun–Thu noon–8pm, Fri and Sat noon–10pm

This local brewery taproom opposite Fort Anne is always buzzing, with regular live performances and a range of beers, from the Big Shot Black IPA to Port Royal Pilsner (plus East Coast Cider).

The Bitter End

1572 Argyle St, Halifax, NS; tel: 902-425 3039; www.bitterend.ca; daily 4pm–2am

Well-known for its martinis, this polished cocktail bar provides a quietly cool beginning to (or end of) a night on the tiles in Nova Scotia's capital.

Copper Bottom Brewing

567 Main St, Montague, PEI; tel: 902-361 2337; www.copperbottombrewing.com; Mon–Thu 1–7pm, Fri and Sat noon–8pm, Sun 1–6pm (seasonal hours)

Best craft beer on Prince Edward Island, with a charming taproom in the old Eastern Graphic building in the small village of Montague, 47km east from Charlottetown. There's fabulous views of the Montague River, an outdoor deck, a range of board games to play and often live music. Try the Blueberry Sour, Nomad Cider, Ken's oatmeal stout or the Juno IPA. It's owned by PEI folk singer-songwriter Ashley Condon and her husband Ken Spears.

Duke of Duckworth Pub

325 Duckworth St (McMurdo's Lane), St John's, NL; tel: 709-739 6344; www.dukeofduckworth.com; Mon–Thu and Sun noon–2am, Fri and Sat noon–3am

Popular bar and Republic of Doyle location, just down the steps off Duckworth St. Serves a wide range of Newfoundland ales (including Quidi Vidi and its own tasty brew, Duke's Own),

Audience at The Carleton

but its speciality is English pints and fish and chips.

Flying Boats Brewing Company
700 Malenfant Blvd, Dieppe (Moncton), NB; https://flyingboatsbrewing.com; Tue–Wed 4–9pm, Thu and Fri noon–9pm, Sat noon–7pm, Sun 1–6pm

Lauded New Brunswick craft brewer, with a taproom that's a little off the beaten path but well worth seeking out. Features live music and friendly service, with long communal tables and stools. The creative beers on offer include Mango Splash Wheat Ale, Red Cap Peanut Butter Stout and Dixie Clipper IPA.

Happinez Wine Bar
42 Princess St, Saint John, NB; tel: 506-634 7340; www.happinezwinebar.com; Wed and Thu 4pm–midnight, Fri 4pm–1am, Sat 5pm–1am.

To take a break from the Maritimes' beer-heavy pub scene, try this intimate wine bar, with exposed brick walls and exceptional wine list. Enjoy the compact "hapito" patio outside in summer, and sample a flight of wines with a selection of charcuterie and cheese plates.

Pump House Brewpub
5 Orange Lane, Moncton, NB; tel: 506-855 2337; www.pumphousebrewpub.ca. Mon–Wed 11am–midnight, Thu 11am–1am, Fri and Sat 11am–2am, Sun noon–midnight.

Popular brewpub that crafts some excellent seasonal beers; if the lauded blueberry cream ale is too fruity, try the hoppy IPA or Muddy River Stout. The pub food is pretty good too (beer bread, beer-steamed mussels, and Moncton's only wood-fired pizza oven).

Live music venues

Bearly's House of Blues
1269 Barrington St, Halifax, NS; tel: 902-423 2526; www.bearlys.ca; Mon–Sat 11am–11pm, Sun 2-11pm.

Near the train station, this low-key bar has regular acts with the emphasis – you guessed it – on blues and bluegrass. Blues jam sessions on Sun nights, often comedy shows on Wed. Also serves excellent BBQ ribs, burgers and cheap pitchers of beer.

The Carleton
1685 Argyle St, Halifax, NS; tel: 902-422 6335, www.thecarleton.ca; Tue, Wed and Sun 4–11pm, Thu 4pm–1am, Fri and Sat 4pm–2am.

One of the best live venues (mostly urban folk) on the East Coast as well as a great bar for wine, proper martinis and draught beer. Also hosts the annual Halifax Urban Folk Festival (Sept), Halifax Jazz Festival in July (www.halifaxjazzfestival.ca) and comedy shows.

Erin's Pub
186 Water St, St John's, NL; tel: 709-722 1916; www.facebook.com/ErinsPubNL;

Pub in St John's NL

daily noon–3am

Popular and well-established no-frills Irish pub, showcasing the best of Newfoundland folk and bluegrass acts Wed–Sun night. It also has the best Guinness in town, as well as ice-cold Black Horse on draught.

Lower Deck

1887 Upper Water St, Halifax, NS; tel: 902-425 1501; www.lowerdeck.ca; May–Sept daily 11.30am–12.30am; Oct–Apr Mon–Wed 5pm–midnight, Thu and Sun 5pm–12.30am, Fri and Sat 11.30am–12.30am.

Traditional Maritime folk music is the speciality in "the Pub" with daily live acts and pub food, while the Beer Market (on the upper floor) reverts to a conventional DJ club at the weekends. Great Big Sea started their career here, and acoustic rock band Signal Hill often performs.

Olde Dublin Pub

131 Sydney St, Charlottetown, PEI; tel: 902-892 6992; www.oldedublinpub. com; Mon–Wed 11am–10pm, Thu 11am–midnight, Fri and Sat 11am–2am, Sun noon–9pm

Intimate and justifiably popular spot with imported and domestic ales, Guinness and Kilkenny included, to accompany the live folk music – mostly Irish – nightly from May to Sept.

The Ship Pub

265 Duckworth St, St John's, NL; tel: 709-753 3870; www.facebook.com/TheShipPubKitchen, Mon–Tue 3pm–1am, Wed noon–1am, Thu noon–2am, Fri–Sun noon–3am.

Down the steps from Duckworth St, this dark, earthy pub showcases an eclectic mix of live music that attracts everyone from grizzled old-timers who love their folk music to arty, black-clad students.

Theatre

Beaverbrook Kin Centre

100 Newcastle Blvd, Miramichi, NB; tel: 506 622 1780; www.miramichifolksongfestival.com.

The former Newcastle town hall and theatre is now best known for hosting the annual Miramichi Folksong Festival (held over five days in early August). It's generally reckoned to be one of the best of its kind, with the focus very much on songs.

Chester Playhouse

22 Pleasant St, Chester, NS; tel: 902-275 3933; https://chesterplayhouse.ca.

Chester – on the coast between Halifax and Lunenburg – is home to this first-rate theatre. Chester Playhouse offers a lively programme of concerts and plays between mid-March and December. It also hosts the Summer Theatre Festival of contemporary music and Canadian-oriented drama, which is held between the months of July and August.

The Masonic Temple building, home to the Spirit of Newfoundland

Confederation Centre of the Arts

145 Richmond St, Charlottetown, PEI;
tel: 902-566 1267, https://confederation
centre.com.

Hosts an extensive variety of acts, from rock and jazz through to comedians, magicians, theatre, opera and ballet. The centre is also the home of the main show of the annual Charlottetown Festival (mid-June to Sept), which is a musical adaptation of Anne of Green Gables, running since 1965.

Grafton Street Dinner Theatre

1741 Grafton St, Halifax, NS; tel: 902-425 1961; https://graftonstdinnertheatre.com; 3–6 shows Tue–Sun, depending on the season, from 6.30–10pm

Music, comedy and interactive characters enhance a traditional Nova Scotian dinner. The shows are usually three-act musical comedies, and the cast regularly interacting with the crowd (the actors double as servers).

Henry House

1222 Barrington St, Halifax, NS; tel: 902-423 5660, www.henryhouse.ca; daily noon–12.45am

British-style pub with a charmingly intimate bar occupying a handsome stone building dating from 1834 – it was once the home of Confederation "father" William A. Henry. Most of the ale is brewed on the premises – try the Peculiar, a fair approximation of the sultry grandeur of the legendary British ale.

Lunar Rogue Pub

625 King St, Fredericton, NB; tel: 506-450 2065; www.lunarrogue.com; Mon–Fri 11am–1am, Sat 10am–1am, Sun 11am–10pm

Popular local bar serving British and Maritime ales as well as an extensive range of malt whiskies. Features live music on most weekends, and a pleasant patio in the summer.

Neptune Theatre

1593 Argyle St, Halifax, NS; tel: 902-429 7070; www.neptune theatre.com.

The doyen of Halifax's live theatres since 1915, offering a wide range of mainstream dramatic productions, from Broadway musicals to plays and Christmas shows. It remains Atlantic Canada's largest professional regional theatre.

Spirit of Newfoundland

6 Cathedral St, St John's, NL; tel: 709-579 3023, www.spiritofnewfoundland.com; June–Sept Tue–Sat 6.30pm; Oct–May usually Fri–Sun only.

The old St John's Masonic Temple is now home to the Spirit of Newfoundland theatre company. The performances that take place here usually feature a Newfoundland theme, with local music and local humour in full effect, and are often combined with dinner. Visiting the Spirit of Newfoundland is a brilliant way to spend an evening in St John's.

The barn and carriage at the Green Gables farmhouse, Cavendish

BOOKS AND FILM

The Atlantic provinces have gradually started to appear more frequently on TV and cinema screens in recent decades, but for such a beautiful part of the world representation remains surprisingly thin. The region has fared slightly better in print, with Lucy Maud Montgomery especially responsible for a good portion of Prince Edward Island's GDP today – her *Anne of Green Gables* books, first published in 1908 and which evoke a beautifully rustic PEI that has barely changed, are still set reading in schools all over the world and are even performed as musical adaptations (at the likes of Charlottetown's Confederation Centre of the Arts) today.

Annie Proulx's *Shipping News* (book published 1993, movie 2003) put Newfoundland on the map, while *Maudie*, which came out in 2006 and stars Sally Hawkins re-ignited interest in Nova Scotian folk artist Maud Lewis. Hugh MacLennan has long been associated with Nova Scotia, with his most notable work, *Two Solitudes*, focusing on English- and Canadian-speaking identities. Meanwhile, French-language author Antonine Maillet has written evocatively about Acadian life in New Brunswick, in well over 20 works.

BOOKS

Fiction (inc poems and plays)
Anne of Green Gables, by L.M. Montgomery. Growing pains and bucolic bliss in a children's classic from 1908, famously set on Prince Edward Island. Led to whole series of sequels, almost all of them also set on PEI.

Barometer Rising by Hugh MacLennan. An evocative depiction of life in Halifax during World War I, and especially the after-effects of the Halifax Explosion of 1917.

Random Passage, by Bernice Morgan. The epic story of an Irishwoman, Mary Brundle, and her perilous odyssey from a harsh English workhouse to the remote Newfoundland outport of Cape Random – a struggling settlement forced to be a community through the sheer will to survive. Followed by *Waiting for Time*. Author Morgan was born in St. John's.

La Sagouine, by Antonine Maillet. The beloved Acadian author's most famous play (and the easiest to find in English translation), is written in Acadian French, as a series of monologues by "la Sagouine", an Acadian cleaning lady from rural New Brunswick.

The Shipping News, by E. Annie Proulx. The 1994 Pulitzer Prize-winner is a rambling, inconclusive narrative of a social misfit who finds love and happiness of sorts in small-town Newfoundland. Superb descriptions of sea, weather and all things waterbound make it an intriguing primer for a visit to the province.

Sally Hawkins as Maud Lewis and Ethan Hawke as Everett Lewis in Maudie

Non-fiction

Cod: A Biography of the Fish that Changed the World, by Mark Kurlansky. This fascinating book tracks the life and times of the cod and the generations of fishermen who have lived off it. There are sections on overfishing and the fish's breeding habits along with cod recipes.

The Dictionary of Newfoundland English, edited by G.M. Story, W.J. Kirwin, and J.D.A. Widdowson. First published in 1982 to widespread acclaim, this historical dictionary focuses on the varieties of English spoken in Newfoundland over the last four centuries. An entertaining book, it offers a wide view of the island's unique culture.

From the Coast to Far Inland-Collected Writings on Labrador, edited by William Rompkey. Excellent collection of rarely seen writing on Labrador, from the Viking Vinland Sagas, to memoirs of pioneers, bush doctors, miners and the Inuit.

Vinland Sagas. The *Saga of the Greenlanders* and *The Saga of Erik the Red* describe the Norse expeditions to North America, beginning in the 10th century – we now know they at least made it as far as at L'Anse aux Meadows in Newfoundland.

FILM AND TV

***Anne of Green Gables**, 1985*. This TV mini-series is still reckoned to be the gold standard of Green Gables depictions, with Megan Follows playing an endearingly spunky Anne Shirley. See also *Anne of Green Gables: The Sequel* (1987). *Anne with an E* (2017–2019) is the Generation Z version.

***The Boys of St. Vincent**, 1992*. TV mini-series based on the sexual abuse scandals that emerged at the Mount Cashel Orphanage in St. John's, Newfoundland, in 1989 – (the facility was closed in 1990).

***Danny**, 2014*. Fascinating documentary about controversial ex-Newfoundland and Labrador premier Danny Williams (who served 2003 to 2010), blending archival footage, dramatic re-enactments and interviews with Williams and his key staff and family members.

***Maudie**, 2016*. Compelling but heartbreaking biopic directed by Aisling Walsh and starring Ethan Hawke and Sally Hawkins as Nova Scotian folk artist Maud Lewis, who had severe arthritis. Controversially filmed in Newfoundland, not Nova Scotia.

***Random Passage**, 2002*. Four-part TV mini-series filmed in Newfoundland, based on two novels written by Bernice Morgan. It's a wonderful evocation of how harsh life was for the early Irish and English settlers.

***The Shipping News**, 2001*. Drama starring Kevin Spacey, Judi Dench and Julianne Moore, based on Annie Proulx's book and mostly shot in and around Trinity, Newfoundland.

***You Are Here: A Come From Away Story**, 2018*. This documentary, directed by Moze Mossanen, tells how Gander, Newfoundland welcomed 6,500 air travellers diverted away from New York on 9/11.

ABOUT THIS BOOK

This *Explore Guide* has been produced by the editors of Insight Guides, whose books have set the standard for visual travel guides since 1970. With top-quality photography and authoritative recommendations, these guidebooks bring you the very best routes and itineraries in the world's most exciting destinations.

BEST ROUTES

The routes in the book provide something to suit all budgets, tastes and trip lengths. As well as covering the destination's many classic attractions, the itineraries track lesser-known sights, and there are also excursions for those who want to extend their visit outside the region. The routes embrace a range of interests, so whether you are an art fan, a gourmet, a history buff or have kids to entertain, you will find an option to suit.

We recommend reading the whole of a route before setting out. This should help you to familiarise yourself with it and enable you to plan where to stop for refreshments – options are shown in the 'Food and Drink' box at the end of each tour.

For our pick of the tours by theme, consult Recommended Routes for… (see pages 6–7).

INTRODUCTION

The routes are set in context by this introductory section, giving an overview of the destination to set the scene, plus background information on food and drink, shopping and more, while a succinct history timeline highlights the key events over the centuries.

DIRECTORY

Also supporting the routes is a Directory chapter, with our pick of where to stay while you are there and select restaurant listings; these eateries complement the more low-key cafés and restaurants that feature within the routes and are intended to offer a wider choice for evening dining. Also included here are some nightlife listings and our recommendations for books and films about the destination.

ABOUT THE AUTHORS

Stephen Keeling worked as a financial journalist for seven years before writing his first travel guide and has since written numerous titles for Rough Guides. Stephen lives in New York City.

CONTACT THE EDITORS

We hope you find this Explore Guide useful, interesting and a pleasure to read. If you have any questions or feedback on the text, pictures or maps, please do let us know. If you have noticed any errors or outdated facts, or have suggestions for places to include on the routes, we would be delighted to hear from you. Please drop us an email at hello@insightguides.com. Thanks!

CREDITS

Explore Maritimes and Newfoundland
Editor: Aimee White
Author: Stephen Keeling
Head of DTP and Pre-Press: Rebeka Davies
Head of Publishing: Sarah Clark
Picture Editor: Tom Smyth
Cartography: Katie Bennett
Photo credits: Avalon 123; Barrett & MacKay Photo/Newfoundland and Labrador Tourism 10, 12, 26, 28/29, 31L, 34, 35, 37, 39L, 38/39, 45, 49L, 54, 64; Battle Harbour Historic Trust 64/65; Baymount Outdoor Adventures Inc. 4ML; Courtsey DestinationLabrador.com 22/23, 61; Dennis Minty/Newfoundland and Labrador Tourism 38; Discover Halifax 6TL, 6MC, 8MR, 14, 16, 18, 69, 70, 104MC, 104MR, 114, 115, 118; Dru Kennedy Photography/Newfoundland and Labrador Tourism 57L, 60, 63; Finn Beales/Newfoundland and Labrador Tourism 56; Gisele's Inn 109; Hecktic Travels I A division of Hecktic Media Inc. 100/101; Marriot 106; Megan McLellan/Newfoundland and Labrador Tourism 107; Michael Winsor/Newfoundland and Labrador Tourism 20, 27, 51; New Brunswick Tourism 8ML, 8MC, 8MC, 15L, 14/15, 17, 20/21, 98, 101L, 102, 104ML, 104MC, 104ML, 117; Newfoundland and Labrador Tourism 4ML, 4MR, 6BC, 7MR, 7M, 19, 24ML, 24/25, 32, 40, 44, 52, 55, 56/57; Nick Hawkins/Tourism New Brunswick 99; O'Brien's Boat Tours 32/33; Paddy Barry/Newfoundland and Labrador Tourism 48/49, 104/105; Ron Hann/Newfoundland and Labrador Tourism 21L; Scott McClellan/Newfoundland and Labrador Tourism 120; Shutterstock 1, 4MC, 4MR, 4MC, 4/5T, 6ML, 7T, 7MR, 8ML, 8MR, 8/9T, 11, 13L, 12/13, 24ML, 24MC, 24MR, 24MC, 24MR, 30, 30/31, 33L, 36, 41, 42/43, 46/47, 48, 50, 53L, 52/53, 58, 59, 62, 65L, 66, 67, 68, 71, 72, 73, 74/75, 76, 77, 78/79, 80, 81, 82, 83L, 82/83, 84, 85L, 84/85, 86, 87L, 86/87, 88, 89, 90/91, 92, 93, 94/95, 96, 97L, 96/97, 100, 103, 104MR, 108, 110, 111, 112, 113, 116, 121, 122; Tourism Nova Scotia 119

Cover credits: St. John's, Newfoundland (main) and a covered bridge in New Brunswick (bottom) both Shutterstock

Printed in China

All Rights Reserved
© 2021 Apa Digital AG
License edition © Apa Publications Ltd UK

First Edition 2021
No part of this book may be reproduced, stored in a retrieval system or transmitted in any form or means electronic, mechanical, photocopying, recording or otherwise, without prior written permission from Apa Publications.

Every effort has been made to provide accurate information in this publication, but changes are inevitable. The publisher cannot be responsible for any resulting loss, inconvenience or injury.

DISTRIBUTION

UK, Ireland and Europe
Apa Publications (UK) Ltd
sales@insightguides.com
United States and Canada
Ingram Publisher Services
ips@ingramcontent.com
Australia and New Zealand
Booktopia
retailer@booktopia.com.au
Worldwide
Apa Publications (UK) Ltd
sales@insightguides.com

SPECIAL SALES, CONTENT LICENSING AND COPUBLISHING

Insight Guides can be purchased in bulk quantities at discounted prices. We can create special editions, personalised jackets and corporate imprints tailored to your needs.
sales@insightguides.com
www.insightguides.biz

INDEX

MAP LEGEND

●	Start of tour
→	Tour & route direction
····	Extra tour
1	Recommended sight
2	Recommended restaurant/café
★	Place of interest
❶	Tourist information
✈ ✈	Airport / Airfield
---	Ferry route
---	Province boundary
🚌	Bus station
Ⓜ	Museum
✚	Church
📖	Library
🎭	Theatre
🗿	Statue
🅿	Parking
🛈	Lighthouse
⚲	Beach
▲	Summit
✳	Viewpoint
	Park
	Important building
	Urban area
	Transport hub
	National park